MW00616233

# *More About Life In The World Unseen*

By
Anthony Borgia

Published by
M.A.P.
272 East 300 North
Midway, UT 84049
(801) 266-4788

ISBN # 0-9636435-2-5

Printed and distributed in the
United States of America by
contract with Fitz Dyer and
U.S.A. 2000.

It has been my privilege and pleasure to act all along as his amanuensis for recording the scripts. Through other sources of communication we have had literally hundreds of forgatherings, where he has brought with him a goodly company of spirit friends.

In the present script, recorded by me in 1951, Monsignor recounts how Ruth and he, but without Edwin on this occasion, embarked upon one of their visits to earth for 'escort duty', in this instance to a young lad of eighteen years. Instead, however, of passing him into the care of other hands, as usually takes place, they invite him to stay with them in their home (where he first awakens to his new life), and thereafter, when fully recovered, they set out upon 'escort duty' of another kind: through the realms in which they live, to see the wonders and meet some of the people.          A.B.

# CONTENTS

# A Passing

You will have read, I hope, the few prefatory words that my earthly amanuensis has written concerning myself, so allowing me to proceed at once to my narrative without going over old ground.

It is now close upon forty years since I stood upon the threshold of a new life when the moment of my dissolution came. During the passage of the last decade I have been enabled to give some account of life as it is lived in these parts of the spirit world wherein I am happy to be living.

Life, you must know, is upon a gigantic scale here in the spirit world, how gigantic you can have very little conception until you yourself come to dwell among us. But because its magnitude is vast that is not to say that it is proportionately complex. Indeed, when one comes to compare the earth world with the spirit world, it is at once apparent how complex the earth world is, and how much simpler is life in the spirit world. This may seem an astonishing statement to make; nevertheless, it is a true one. That, however, is a subject which I will discuss with you later. And now, without further preamble, to my narrative.

Situated in the city, which is not far from my home here, is a large building which carries out the important functions of an office of records and inquiries. Here knowledge is to be obtained upon an infinite range and variety of subjects and affairs. Of all these, what closely interests us at the moment is that department which deals with the actual passing of folk from the earth to the spirit world. Part of my work consists of helping people at the moment of their physical death, people of all kinds, of both sexes, of any religion—or none—and of all ages, from young folk to the aged. Working in conjunction with me are my two old friends, Edwin and Ruth. Sometimes Edwin is not with us, but Ruth and I almost always work together.

Now you may wonder how we come to know when our services are needed, and who or what directs those services into the required quarter. The answer is a simple one: the office of records and inquiries. It is not part of our normal actions to be fully acquainted with all or any of the methods employed in the gathering of information by this central office. All that Ruth and I are called upon to do is apprise this office with the fact that we are both free to undertake whatever task may present itself, and we follow the simple procedure of awaiting notification that our services are desired.

We were seated, then, upon a particular occasion in our house, which is itself a replica of my old home on earth, when word reached us that our presence was desired at the central office. We at once proceeded thither, and were greeted by one whom we had come to know very well during the passage of years, as he had come to know us.

This man is a genial soul, of great kindness and comprehension, and his knowledge of those who work for him is prodigious. For it is by the application of this knowledge that he is enabled to send upon their various missions those of us who are exactly suited to the specific task in hand.

There may appear to be a great similarity between one normal transition and another when viewed by earthly eyes, .but from our point of view the variations are enormous. They are as great, in fact, as the variations in human personalities. What to the earthly beholder is the end of life, is to us and the person chiefly concerned, the beginning of a new one. It is with the personality that we have to deal, and according to the personality, to the knowledge or ignorance of spiritual matters of the passing soul, so is our especial task governed and our course of action regulated. In short, every 'death' is treated and served with strict regard to its essential requirements. So that we are allotted our various tasks with one eye, as it were, upon our capabilities, experience, temperament, and so on. Edwin, Ruth and I are decidedly of similar temperament, while our capabilities and experience have been augmented and broadened by long practice.

As you can imagine, a great deal of patience has at times to be exercised when we are confronted with minds that are tenacious of old beliefs and ideas that bear no relationship with the truth and facts and realities of spirit life, and it may take much arduous work to free the newly arrived person of so much that is mentally inhibiting and spiritually retarding. You will see, then, the wisdom of choosing instruments who are ably suited in all respects to the work in hand, so that a difficult or awkward case may not be rendered more so.

The spirit world never does things by halves, to use a familiar expression, and what might appear to be sheer preciosity to the incarnate is clear wisdom to us who have to carry out the work. No trouble is spared. We have infinity of time, a vast amount of patience, together with the services of a multitude of people always available. There is no bungling, there are no mistakes; nothing is left to chance. Our principal in the central office, therefore, knowing us, sends us upon our missions to earth with complete confidence in his choice of ourselves, while for our part, we have complete confidence that we are not being given a task beyond our powers of performance.

After a few friendly exchanges and kindly inquiries, our friend turned to the business in hand. A perfectly straightforward case, he informed us, and one that should present no unusual features. 'It is the passing,' he said, 'of a lad, aged eighteen. A sprightly youth; mentally alert and receptive. I have kept this case for you both, as I think he will be useful to you later on when he has become accustomed to things. Would you care to take him to your home? It would be a good plan.' We readily acquiesced.

We then plied our friend with a few questions so that we should be as fully charged with information as possible. It appeared that the lad's earthly end was approaching rapidly, that he had no prejudices concerning the subject of 'life after death'; his religious instruction had followed the usual lines but had not left any very great impression. There was a happy toleration between him and his parents, but no such strong affection as would introduce any complications of an emotional nature. The parents would regard the early 'death' of their son as part of God's will, and they would therefore submit in accordance thereto.

We were agreed that this certainly did seem to be a straightforward case enough, and we were not sorry, inasmuch as we had a number of very trying transitions of late, and welcomed this fresh one upon easier lines.

You will no doubt wonder how we are directed at the outset of our 'labours' to the actual 'chamber of death', to use a most lugubrious phrase. Incidentally, what a wealth of gloom and lamentation it conjures up! It seems as though all the most doleful phrases are specially reserved for the simple act of passing from your world to ours. Of course you do not need to remind me that from the point of view of those who are parting from a loved one, it is no time for cheerfulness and 'joy abounding'. Yet were the truth known and realized, what a world of difference it would make, especially if that happy state of things were to exist to the end that all the mournful trappings so closely associated with transition were to be ruthlessly cast out. Is not the event, at the present day, sufficiently harrowing in itself without adding to its gloom by the adoption of so much black? This, I am afraid, is a slight digression. To return.

We are given the name, but not the address of the person upon whom we are to attend. Indeed, the whole procedure is far simpler, and gives a very good example of what I mentioned but a moment ago regarding the relative simplicity of life in our world as compared with the complexities of life in yours. Everything, you will say, must have a beginning, so that some indication must be given somewhere *by* someone *to* someone that the passing of a particular person is about to take place, within, shall we say, a matter of an hour or two of earthly time. It is hardly likely, things being what they are, that a direct message would be sent out to us from earth people intimating that assistance was required at an imminent dissolution.

It is not my purpose, at this moment, to trace matters to their source, and, strictly speaking, we who undertake this kind of work are not concerned with the minutiæ of organization which terminate with our presenting ourselves at the side of the passing soul. That is part of the expert economic functions that are but a commonplace in spirit lands. This, however, can be said: the knowledge that a transition is about to take place, together with its precise location, is the result of a remarkable conveyance of information, passed from one to another, commencing with that important functionary, the individual's personal spirit guide, and terminating with us who undertake the work of escorting folk from the earth world to their homes in the spirit world. Between the former and the latter there is a clear concatenation of minds, if I may so express it, an exchange of information carried out by thought transmission, accurately and rapidly.

At the present moment, as Ruth and I were seated before our friend of the central office, all that remained was to receive our 'sailing directions'. These were given to us in this manner: our friend sent a message—by thought, of course—to the spirit person who was in attendance at the place of dissolution, to the effect that we were ready to assume charge whenever he deemed it advisable. This brought an instantaneous response. We could perceive the light as it flashed to our friend, and by a sort of confluence we were brought into the 'thought-beam'. We were now in direct *rapport* with our attendant friend 'at the other end', as you would say. And now—to use very unscientific language—we had but to project ourselves along this thought-beam to find ourselves in the exact spot where our services were needed. How this happens, I have not the remotest notion. All that Ruth or I could tell you is what we do, how we do it, but not *how* it *happens*! Do you believe you could describe in simple terms—or any terms—precisely what you do when you think, and having done that, tell me how it happens? Try that 'simple' experiment for yourselves, and then you will understand just what I mean!

We now thanked our principal for this new case, and upon his intimation that the time was close at hand, we immediately set forth.

Ruth and I found ourselves in a bedroom of a house of modest dimensions, unpretentious, and moderately prosperous as far as earthly possessions were concerned. A nurse was in attendance, and relatives were close at hand. It was evident that they believed the end was not far distant, and the doctor appeared to have done all that he could to make things easier for his patient.

There also seemed to be some evidence that a minister of their church had not long left the room. There were distinct signs that prayerful petitions had been sent forth, but these being couched in the usual terms of theological obscurity, and in addition being totally inapposite to the events about to take place, they were completely ineffective to achieve any purpose whatever beyond giving a doubtful satisfaction to those then present. This was a matter, however, that Ruth and I were quickly able—and qualified—to set right. We did so, asking for a downflowing of helpful power to supplement our own natural resources and abilities. It was instantly forthcoming, and was clearly observable in the bright beams of light that diffused themselves round about us.

It was plain to see that in a brief space our friend would be joining us. Accordingly, we commenced our small preparations. Ruth stationed herself at the head of the bed within easy reach of the lad's head, and placing her hands upon his brow, she gently smoothed his temples.

We are never certain that our ministrations are perceived or felt unless the 'patient' reveals some sign or another that he—or she—has done so. In this case, it was patent that Ruth was making a decided impression, because coincidental with her placing her hands upon the boy's head, he turned his eyes with an upward motion as though seeking or trying to per-ceive whence the pleasant, soothing sensation came.

It was possible that he could actually see Ruth; if that were the case, so much the better.

We had both assumed a replica of our former earthly habiliments, Ruth being attired in a gay summery garment, looking very natural and normal, and altogether charming. It is necessary to emphasize this, since it was—and always is—our aim to appear as unlike 'celestial beings', should our presence be observed, as it is possible to be. (When Edwin came to meet me upon my own transition, he revealed himself to me dressed in his customary earthly attire. Had he pre-sented himself to me in his spirit clothes, there is every reason to believe that I should have been sufficiently terrified to fancy that if the worst had not come, it could not be long delayed!)

I perched myself at the foot of the lad's bed, and directed my gaze upon him, and there were evident signs of his seeing me. I smiled to him, and gently waved my hand to reassure him. So far, things were proceeding very favourably—would that all passings were as serene.

The great moment in the boy's life had now arrived. I moved to a position at about the middle of the bed upon the side opposite to Ruth. The boy had lapsed into a gentle sleep. As he did so, his spirit body rose slowly above his inert physical body to which it was attached by a bright silver cord—the lifeline as it is termed. I placed my arms beneath the floating form; there was the slightest momentary twitch, the cord detached itself, retracted, and disappeared.

To the relatives in the bed-chamber, the boy was 'dead' and 'gone'. To Ruth and me he was *alive* and *present*.

I held him in my arms, as one would a child, while Ruth again placed her hands upon his head. A gentle movement of her hands for a minute or two to ensure that the boy would be peacefully comfortable, and we were ready to start upon our rapid journey to our home.

Throughout the transit Ruth held one of the boy's hands, thus giving him energy and strength while I supported him in my arms. The journey, as with all such journeys, was soon over; we had left the dismal bedroom, and we were in our own beautiful land and home. Quietly and gently we laid the boy upon a very comfortable couch, Ruth seating herself close beside him, as I took a chair at the foot facing our new arrival. 'Well, my dear,' Ruth remarked with evident satisfaction, 'I really think he'll do.' All there was for us to do now, was to await the awakening, which, in the nature of the case, would not be long delayed.

Our simple, but usually effective, arrangements had already been made. The couch upon which the lad had been laid, was placed close beneath a wide open window in such a position that, without even the slightest movement of the head, a most enchanting view was to be seen of the gardens without, while through a gap in a line of trees, a distant view of our beautiful city was to be had, clear and colourful. Upon the wall immediately facing the lad there hung a large mirror, so that the reflection of the rest of the room, with all that it suggested in comfort and ease, could be observed with the merest turn of the eye. Children's voices could be heard in the distance, and the birds were singing with their customary vigour.

This was the pleasant situation awaiting out friend when he emerged from his short but refreshing sleep, and this is often the moment when our *real* work begins!

# The Awakening

RUTH was the first to speak when our friend had opened his eyes.

'Well, Roger,' she said, 'how do you feel?' (Our friend at the office had given us the boy's first name, which was sufficient for all purposes.)

Roger opened his eyes still wider as he turned to Ruth. 'Why,' said he, 'I saw you—when was it? A little while ago. Who are you?'

'Just a friend to help you. Call me Ruth.'

'And you, sir. I seem to remember you were sitting at the foot of my bed.'

'That's right,' I said. 'The memory will become clearer in a moment or two.'

Roger started to sit upright, but Ruth gently pressed him back upon the cushions. 'Now, Roger,' said she, 'the order of the day is that you just stay quietly there, and not do too much talking.'

The boy stared out of the window.

'Lovely view, isn't it,' I said, pointing through the window. 'Feeling comfortable? That's right. Well, now, you are wondering what all this is about. Have you any idea what has happened? Only a hazy notion. But the great thing is that now you are feeling all right. All the aches and pains gone. Isn't that it?'

Roger nodded and smiled as the realization seemed to come upon him. 'Yes, rather, thank you.'

The boy was obviously not of the nervous sort, and there appeared to be no purpose in withholding the truth any longer. I caught Ruth's eye, and she nodded in agreement.

'Roger, my dear boy,' I began, 'I have some pleasant news for you. You were perfectly correct, you did see Ruth and me a little while ago. We were in your bedroom at home, and you were very ill, so ill that the doctor couldn't pull you through. So Ruth and I came to bring you through, into another world, a lovely world. Do you follow?'

'Then, I've died. Is that it?'

'That's it, old fellow. You're not frightened?'

'No, 1 don't think so.' He paused. 'I never expected anything like this' he added.

'No, I don't suppose you did. Who does, except the very comparative few who know what's to come? Honestly, now, what did you expect?'

'Goodness only knows.'

'Angels with large wings, and stern countenances, looking very frigid and remote? Suppose you had seen something like that, what would you have felt and thought? You needn't tell me; I'll answer the question for you. You would have thought that they had come to haul you off to be tried before some awful Judge somewhere in the High Court of Heaven. And woe betide you if you had misbehaved yourself, my lad.'

Ruth gave a merry peal of laughter, while Roger, who had caught the look in my eye and interpreted it correctly, laughed too.

'Let me tell you at once, Roger, that there are no judges, or even a single great judge, anywhere in this world, the spirit world. Any judging to be done, we do it for ourselves, and manage very nicely. You'll find you will become extremely critical of yourself, as we all do. We can be very hard on ourselves even. So whatever you may have thought about Judgment Day, dismiss the whole idea from your mind. There is no such thing, there never has been, and *there never will be.*

'Now I expect you are wondering what is to happen next,' I went on. 'The answer to that is simple: Nothing!—at least for a little while, until you feel refreshed, and then we might all go off together and explore things a bit. How does that appeal to you?'

'It appeals to me very much, but there is something I would like to know.' Roger looked round. 'Whose house is this, and who are you? I can see you are a padre, but the colour of your cassock is not what I've ever seen before.'

'As to the house, it is mine, though really it is ours, as Ruth lives most of her time with me and so does an old clergyman friend you will meet later. As to my clothes, these I am wearing are only replicas of my earthly ones which I have put on specially for you. I have proper spirit clothes, but suppose I had worn them—and Ruth hers—when we came to fetch you in your room, we might have looked like those grim, forbidding angels I spoke about just now. And no matter how we set our faces into pleasant looks and smiles, there is no doubt there would have been a very frightened Roger. So, behold us as we used to be when we lived on earth, and now you look at yourself as you used to be on earth only a very short while ago.'

Roger glanced down at his clothes to discover that he was wearing a pair of flannel trousers and a brown jacket, while on his feet were a pair of substantial shoes. He caught hold of the material as thought to reassure himself that it was real. He even clutched his arm to make doubly sure he was solid! Then he placed one foot on the floor and stamped lightly with it.

'All pretty solid, eh, Roger?'

From a side-table Ruth fetched a huge bowl of fruit, and offered it to the boy. 'You'll find these very real, too,' said she with a smile; 'help yourself to what you fancy. They're lovely, and will do you a world of good. We keep them here "specially".'

We all three took some fruit, and Ruth and I waited to see the boy tackle his. First, he looked at it closely, turning it over and over in his hand—it was a plum he was examing—and seemed undecided what to do with it. There is, of course, only one thing to do with a fine, juicy plum, especially if it is one grown in the spirit world, and that is to eat it. Ruth and I did so, while Roger watched closely to see what would happen. He expected, no doubt, to see a torrent of juice run out and down our clothes. His eyes opened in astonishment when he saw the juice run out, certainly, and with equal certainty, disappear, leaving our clothes unstained. Thus encouraged, he followed our example, and was wild with delight at this seeming wizardry.

'Nothing is wasted here, Roger,' explained Ruth; 'everything that is unwanted returns to its source. Nothing is destroyed. You couldn't destroy anything however hard you tried. If you find you no longer need or desire a thing it will simply fade away to all appearances, just evaporate before your eyes. But it is not lost; it will return to the source from which it came. If we didn't want this house and all its contents, it would vanish, and there would be nothing to see but the ground it stood on. It's the same with anything else you care to name. All things are living in the spirit world; we don't have such things as "inanimate objects". Things are managed much better here than on the old earth, don't you think—from the tiny bit you've seen of things so far?'

Roger thanked Ruth for her explanation. He seemed a little diffident in the matter of speaking, though, of course Ruth had recommended him not to talk too much yet. However, he turned to me after pondering Ruth's words, with something of an air of puzzlement:

'Were you a bishop, or something?' he asked.

'Oh dear, no,' I laughed; 'nothing so grand or exalted. You were going by the colour of this garment I'm wearing. No, I was only Monsignor when I was on earth. Some of my friends there still call me by the old title. It pleases them, and does no harm, though really we have no such titles and distinguishing marks here. Still, if you would like to use the same name, do so by all means. It serves a useful purpose, and it's not "against the regulations". Ruth always uses it.'

Here I would like to interpolate one or two observations which I think it expedient to make. What I am setting down is the account of an actual case, a real occurrence, though it is typical of many. The young lad, Roger, is a person of real existence, who came into the spirit world in the circumstances precisely as I am now giving you.

Again: exception may be taken to the conversation as I have recounted it to you. There are folk who will object that the whole of it is too appallingly flippant and trivial to merit consideration for one moment; that it is frivolous and third-rate, and such as would not, most certainly *not* be indulged in in any region that could be properly designated 'heaven'; that 'heaven' must surely be conducted upon lines far less commonplace and far more holy and spiritual.

It may be complained that anyone making 'the awful change' from life to death and from death to eternal life— 'supernatural' life—would have far graver things to think about and discuss than the conversational fripperies which I 'allege' take place.

With a long experience of transitions upon which to draw, commencing with *my own*, I know this beyond peradventure: when the last earthly breath has been drawn, and life has begun in the spirit world, there is never the slightest inclination, at that vital moment, to think in terms of learned theological disquisitions or indulge in any 'pious platitudes'.

Every soul who arrives in these or other realms of the spirit world completely untutored about life here, is concerned with one thing and one thing only: what is to happen next? Just that. Because we are inhabitants of the spirit world we have not become grand rhetoricians, who speak only in long eloquent periods upon matters of the highest spiritual consideration. *Deo gratias* that we do not. We are normal, rational people, who speak and act in a normal, rational manner.

Suppose Ruth and I in taking charge of Roger, had adopted a grave comportment and grim countenances, what do you imagine would have happened both to him and us? The lad would have been terrified, where, in good truth, no grounds for fear existed, and all for what purpose? Merely so that Ruth and I should appear and act as misguided folk *believe* we should appear and act, as became inhabitants of the world of spirit.

And what would have happened to Ruth and me? We should have been adjudged totally unfitted for the occupation we had adopted, and at once sent upon our way—*in disgrace*. However, such a thing could never transpire, since we should not be entrusted with this work were we to harbour such unthinkable notions. So it is, my dear friends, that in our conversation with Roger, *as with thousands of others* upon whom we have attended, we are just ourselves. After all, this is a world of life and activity and truth, not a sham, shadowy, sanctimonious mockery of existence. How glad we all are that it is so! We prefer our form of 'heaven' to the strange conception current in some quarters on earth. Now to return to my narrative.

Roger had felt tempted to rise from his couch, a sure sign that he was gaining in strength and vigour. The fruit had made an improvement, as we knew it would. In matters of that kind there are no failures. At the same time, it would not have done to let him test his strength too far, and so for the time being, commended he should remain where he was. He was—and of course, still is!—a most amiable fellow, and was ready to fall in with all our suggestions. In such cases as these, that is, in the initial moments of the newly arrived, so much depends upon the little incidents, those homely things, of great implication in themselves, and outwardly so very reassuring—and comforting.

Long experience has taught us that often the smallest, most insignificant incident can do far more to bring peace and mental quietude to the newcomer to spirit lands than would a hundred of the most brilliant dissertations. Therefore it is that we deliberately introduce the apparently trivial. And I cannot do better to exemplify this than by recounting what next occurred in our care of Roger.

The boy suddenly turned his gaze towards the window, attracted by the sound of fluttering wings upon the window, when he perceived a small bird had made its entrance into the room, and had perched itself only a foot or so from him. Roger remained perfectly still, as though scarcely daring to move lest he should frighten the small visitor away. Ruth, however, called to the bird, which immediately flew to her and perched upon her outstretched finger. The bird was dressed in a smart livery of pale grey feathers.

Roger was greatly interested when Ruth transferred the bird to his own finger.

'He often visits us here,' I told him, 'though he really belongs to two old earth friends of mine.'

'Then what is he doing here?' asked Roger.

'Well, he was found by my friends in great distress when he was a fledgeling; they cared for him, watched him grow, but sad to say, he came to grief. Possibly he became a trifle too daring, overdid things, had some sort of sudden seizure, and died almost at once. A great pity. He was like you, Roger, young and had hardly begun his life. And exactly like you, Roger, he passed into these beautiful lands, and was cared for immediately, just as we try to do for all the human souls who come to us. That small bird, so very inconsiderable on earth, and the action of my two friends, equally inconsiderable, have not been lost. Their affection for that tiny atom of life has preserved that life for all time. At present he is part of the "household" of a mutual old friend, who already has other bird and animal friends of his own. They're a merry family, and we'll take you along to see him—and them. Don't you think he is a rather handsome fellow ?'

'I do. What kind of bird is he?'

'When he first came to us here, he was a much darker grey, and not so big. But he has grown, and his colour, as you see, is now almost dove-grey. What kind of bird is he, did you say? Why only a common sparrow.'

Ruth was indignant that I should refer to him as in any sense common, and so I was compelled to recant—not for the first time since I came to the spirit world!

Roger was still playing with the bird, when Ruth espied two visitors coming towards the house. They were walking in leisurely fashion through the garden, often stopping to examine the flowers that were growing in profusion round the house. As they drew nearer, we recognized them as old friends who had often come to see us before. One, the taller of the two, was a Chaldean by nationality, the other an Egyptian.

I told Roger that not on any account was he to rise when these two visitors came into the room, as they both knew the purpose for which that couch was used, for it had had many and many a newly arrived person resting upon it. Ruth and I went to the door to .welcome our visitors, and cordial greetings were exchanged. The Chaldean's name is Omar, by which he is universally known. He is a man of striking appearance, the most remarkable feature being his raven-black hair, so much in contrast with the slight pallor of his complexion. He is, without doubt, one of the merriest souls to be met with in these lands, and he has a wide reputation for his keen sense of humour.

'Will you come in, Omar,' I said, 'and see our "patient"?' He replied they would be delighted, and we moved two chairs nearer the couch.

'Well, my son, how are you feeling? Happy? Rested?' Omar turned to us: 'Roger is wondering who I am. Perhaps he is wondering what I am.'

'You see, Omar, you are really the first person he has seen waring spirit clothes. Isn't that so, Roger?'

'Yes, it is, and well, I'm a bit confused. Your clothes,' he said to Omar, 'are so different from Monsignor's.'

'Different from those he is wearing now because he did not want to frighten you. You are not frightened of me, are you Roger? There's no need to be, my dear son, for I'm really harmless, and my two friends—your two friends—will vouch for me.  Perhaps you think I'm an angel.  Well, that's better than being thought a devil.  Do you know, Roger, there are some charming people on earth who would call me one, yes, and you, too; in fact, all of us here!  Do you think Ruth looks particularly satanic?  Monsignor, now; there is certainly a hint of brimstone about *him*.  Well, well, it's a good thing we can laugh though, mind you, those same nice people would deny us that.  Speaking for myself, I don't feel the least bit holy, and Monsignor is far too hardened a sinner ever to come within a mile of it.'

Omar turned to me: 'I must be off now,' said he, 'give my love to my friends on earth.'  Then he took Roger by the hand, held it for a moment, and patted him on the cheek.  'Bless you, my son,' he said, 'be rested, then get your friends to show you the glories of these lands.  This is your own home land, now, you know.  And just between ourselves, we're rather proud of it.'

# A First View

As WE returned to the house after parting with Omar and his companion, we saw that Roger had left his couch and was now leaning out of the window. We waved to him, and he waved back.

'It looks as though he's completely regained his vigour,' I remarked to Ruth.

'There's no doubt of it, I should say.'

'And I should say what's completed his "cure" is Omar's visit. Did you notice how he held the boy's hand? If that wasn't charging him with vitality I'm much mistaken. Now isn't that just like Omar.'

There was no question that a great change had been wrought in the lad for he stood in the doorway as we drew near with every appearance of youthful buoyancy. No longer was that slight languidness to be seen, so common in such cases.

'Well, Roger,' said Ruth, 'you look ready for anything.'

'That's how I do feel, Ruth. Now, Monsignor, the old brain has got clear, and I want to know lots of things.' He grasped an arm of each of us, and held us in a firm grip.

'Omar certainly *has* given you strength, judging by the pressure,' I observed. He laughed, and it was good to hear him, for it showed more than anything else could, that the lad was now clearly himself, and that our task thenceforward would be the simple one of introducing him to the wonders of the spirit world, always an enjoyable occupation, in spite of the fact that we had gone through a similar performance times without number

'Come along, my boy, and let's start on the roof.'

'On the roof? What on earth do we want to go climbing on the roof for?'

'On earth, Roger, my lad, no reason at all. However, I know what you mean. Come along and wait till you get there before making any rude remarks about it. Now then, to the roof!'

We mounted the stairs to the upper floor. Here there is a passage, and about half-way along it is a small bay, in which a brief flight of stairs leads to a door on to a flat roof. Here was presented to the astonished gaze of Roger a most superb view of the countryside, a vast territory extending far away into the distance.

'Now, Roger; cast your eyes over this. Did you ever see anything like it, or even remotely approaching it in beauty?'

The boy was silent for a minute or two as he turned in a full circle. 'Gracious heavens,' he said.

'And that's just about it,' said Ruth, 'those two words are a complete description, if ever there was one.'

'Now, Monsignor, Ruth—I don't care which of you—but one of you must tell me what all this is. All those people, for instance. What are they doing?'

We could see many people interspersed about the countryside, some close at hand, others at a distance; some in small
groups, others in larger, and individuals either seated or
walking alone.

'All these folk you see are going about their various
business, or perhaps no definite business at all. Look there at
that little group sitting beneath the big tree. They may be
doing all manner of things, from merely having a pleasant,
gossipy chat among friends, or perhaps one of them is doing
what Ruth and I are now doing for you—introducing you to
the spirit world. Whatever it is all these folk are doing, no one
will tell them they shouldn't be doing it—and move them on!

'Of absolute positive idling, I don't think you'll find a
trace, Roger, because no one, as far as I've been able to find
out—and Ruth and I have poked about in all sorts of places—
no one ever feels the slightest inclination to do nothing simply
by virtue of an indolent nature. There *are* no indolent natures
here. We are always occupied in some way, but that doesn't
mean that this is a life of eternal work as opposed to the *old*—
and still current—idea of eternal rest. We all, every one of us,
have our time off, and no one will come and tell us it's time to
start work again in the earthly sense. We have all the
recreation we need and desire, and we come and go as we
please. What Ruth and I are doing now, here on this roof, is
a very pleasant form of recreation to us both, and a pleasant
change from our chief occupation. It might look as though we
were idling the time away—to anyone who didn't know. But,
you know, Roger, there are millions of us here—with no
over-crowding either, as you can see—so that even as there's
plenty to do, there are plenty of people to do it.'

'Well, that's simple enough, Monsignor, but that makes
me wonder what I'm going to do.'

'Then stop wondering, my dear,' put in Ruth. 'Good gracious, why you've only just arrived here. Wait till you've been here as long as we have, then you'll see there's not always such a terrific hurry to be getting on with something.'

'How long have you been here, then Ruth'

'Oh, getting on for forty years.'

'And you, Monsignor'

'About the same time. There might be ten minutes difference between us! You see we are really seasoned residents.'

'How long has Omar been here?'

Ruth and I exchanged glances, and there was a roar of laughter.

'Omar has been in the spirit world some two thousand years, Roger. I think I had better withdraw what I said about being seasoned residents.'

The lad enjoyed our trifling joke, and so was helped along the road of self-assurance and well-being.

'Now, Ruth, point out the sights to Roger.'

'Do you see that large building with the blue beam of light coming down on it? That's a home of rest for people immediately after they have arrived here. You could have gone there. It's very beautiful, and you would have been well looked after, with every kindness in the world.'

'Then why was I brought here?'

'You're not sorry, are you?'

'No, *no;* I could never be that.'

'The suggestion of bringing you here came from the particular person who sends us on our various errands in helping folk, when they are crossing into this world. He thought it would be a good idea, and we shouldn't dream of questioning his wisdom. It would not be the first time this has happened, by any means; many people have caught their first peep of the spirit world while reclining on that couch down-stairs. It is good for them, and it is good for us.'

Roger pointed to the houses of all kinds that could be seen, some almost buried among the trees, others in more open ground. 'Whose are those?' he asked.

'They belong to the folk here. Once you have the right to possess a home there is nothing to prevent you from having one. Everything is owned upon the same terms here, no matter what it is—even your spirit clothes. That does not mean that you might have to walk abroad naked, because by some mischance you had not earned the right to possess clothes! The natural laws here work in a rational way.'

I broke into the conversation: 'It's not by any means everyone who owns a house here, Roger. Some people don't want to be bothered with one—though bothered is not the exact word to use, as no home, whether large or small, can possibly be any bother in the old earthly sense. But there are folk who don't feel the necessity for a house, and so they don't have one. Perfectly simple. To begin with, the sun is always shining in these and other regions, there's no unpleasant wind or cold. It's always the same steady, unvarying, genial warmth you can feel now. So there's nothing from which we need protection as on earth, in the way of the elements. As for privacy, well, there are myriads of spots—you can see some of them from here—that will provide all the solitude you are ever likely to want.'

'What are those large buildings in the far distance?' our friend asked.

'Those are the various halls of learning in the city. In fact, that *is* the city. Everything in the way of knowledge is to be found somewhere there, and a thousand accomplishments can be gained there. You can become a technician in any of the varied occupations that are all part of the life of the spirit world.'

So we went on, pointing out innumerable things to Roger, explaining this, providing reasons for that, and bringing a clearer understanding to a young mind that had left the earth—as so many do—with no knowledge whatever of the most important part of the Universe—the spirit world. He could see, spread out before him into seemingly illimitable space, the stupendous countryside, with the bright verdure, the rich coulours abounding upon all sides, the gentle undulations leading to the glistening water of lake or river. The carefully laid-out gardens, the flowers, the birds, all heavenly nature—with the blue sky above.

I suggested that we now move downstairs. Roger admired the neatness and solid comfort of the various rooms he peeped into on the way down, and when we had at last reached the lower room that he now knew so well, he broached a matter that we could see was on his mind.

'Where, Monsignor, shall I have to live?'

'You won't *have* to live anywhere in particular, Roger,' I answered. 'You may live where you like, though I understand you have no house of your own. You could have one if you wished, but do you? It would be rather like living in solitary state, although you would have plenty of visitors one way and another. You couldn't really be lonely here, and you have but to step outside your door to find people who would soon drive any loneliness away. Still, Ruth and I know what you mean, so I would like to make this suggestion if it falls in with your own ideas in the matter. Would you care to live in this house with us? You see the size of it—there's plenty of room, and to spare. There are all sorts of little things to interest you, without having to go outside. Stay here for as long as you wish, and be sure of one thing: never will you outstay your welcome.

'We cannot foresee the absolute future, and time, as you will have guessed by now, is of little consideration. Ruth and I, with Edwin, whom you've not met yet, have been doing this work, among other things, for years now. We seem likely to continue for more and more years yet. We are none of us tired of it. Even so, if we changed our work, we should still wish to have our house here.

'Spiritual progression is another matter, Roger. When we go higher—or farther along the road—we may move into other quarters. We need not think of that at present. Join our small household. In other words, stay where you are. That shouldn't be difficult as you have no "goods and chattels".'

The boy started to express his gratitude, but we stopped him. There was no need for words; his thoughts were sufficient.

'That's settled, then,' said Ruth, 'and now, Roger, tell us what *you* think of things.'

Our friend seated himself in a comfortable chair, and looked considerably puzzled. 'What I can't make out,' he said, at length, 'is how all this you've shown me squares up with religion I wasn't taught much, and never knew exactly what to expect. . . .'

'You're not the first to wonder that, Roger. Millions do the same. Ruth and I did so. We were in no better case than yourself. What it comes to is this: when you are on earth, this whole spirit world is regarded as the "life after death", the "next world", and is treated solely from the religious stand-point, except by a comparatively *select* few. I call them select because those few possess the truth—not all the truth, natu-rally , but sufficient for absolute comfort. The religions of the earth have assumed rights over this life to which they are not entitled. The passing from earth to the spirit world is not a religious affair whatever. It's a purely natural process, and one that cannot be avoided. Living a good life on earth is not a religious matter. Why should it be? Have you seen signs of that sort of thing here, Roger  Yet who will dare to say we are not living good, decent lives here?

'Then take the total number of religions on earth. There are thousands among the Christians alone, and all believing something different from each other.'

'I read somewhere that no one religion possessed all the truth, but that each had a bit of it, so that taken all together they'd have the truth between them. Isn't that so, Monsignor?'

'That is so. I've heard of that theory, but think what it involves. First, how are you going to tell what is the truth among all the rest of the claims of any one particular Church. Is one to be content with that one fragment, if it can be discovered, or try to do the impossible, and join all the religious bodies spread over the earth, and so become possessed of all the truth—though you'd have the deuce of a job in sorting the false sheep from the truthful goats?'

The boy gave a loud laugh.

'You can laugh, Roger, my boy, but that's what it comes to in the end.'

'Sitting here in this chair, in this room, actually in the spirit world seems an awful long way from sitting in a church on Sunday, as I used to—sometimes.'

'Only sometimes?' put in Ruth; 'that was naughty in one so young!'

'I know what you're thinking of,' I said; 'that Sunday church-going, with the clergyman, and the choir singing, and the sermon—and the collection, don't forget that! Especially the sermons that didn't seem to have any bearing on what you know *now*. How could it have, coming from the average minister? How could you expect a person—or a parson—to be able to instruct others on a particular subject, or on any subject, when the instructor knows literally nothing about it? That's the real trouble. Ignorance, or lack of knowledge. Yet it is his job, the minister's job, to know. *I* should have known, but I didn't. A person in my position on earth should have been able to tell a person in Ruth's position, or yours, Roger, all that we know at this moment. There are abundant opportunities for finding out.

'What a mournful, miserable business it all is, when you come to think about it. Here is this magnificent world we're living in, and yet on earth it has been shrouded and obscured with a multitude of extraordinary beliefs, conditions, limitations, misconceptions, and I don't know what else besides. The one cannot be reconciled with the other. Like oil and water, they do not mix. Unlike those two substances, there is nothing with which to emulsify them, so to speak. They are not to be fused.

'Odd, isn't it, how the religions of the earth have assumed authority over us—so they think? They cannot regard us in terms of solid reality, of rational living, of breathing, working, playing, helping one another. They would look upon that bird you have there, Roger, as being too outrageous, too preposterous to bear thinking about, even remotely. Yet that little grey fellow is part of life in these lands, and a beautiful part of it, too. How many folk have their animal friends on earth as part of their very lives? Thousands, but the same thing would be denied us here, if some people on earth had their way. It's not *religious*; it's not what one would look for in spiritual realms. It's not the kind of thing that God would allow, because it's too *earthly* and frivolous. It brings us back to that appalling angel I spoke to you about, Roger, when you had opened your eyes as you lay on the couch.

'The whole thing can be summed up in this way, Roger, my boy: the earthly religions know nothing about this world at all, about the life we live.  They do not seem to be able to conjure up in their minds any sort of vision or image of what it might conceivably be.  But they are certain of what it cannot be—upon what authority no one knows—that it cannot be anything like *this* at all.  No man on earth would be prepared to suggest—if he were sane—that the only thing too look forward to is a life of doing nothing for all eternity, in a place or region that was simply vaporous, a void.  The very thought of such an existence—and it would be barely that—would fill him with deep horror, and decide him that he would not *wish* to survive under such ghastly conditions.  And no one could blame him.

'Now, Roger, let's go out and do a little visiting.  Bring the bird with you.  He could show you the way, without us.  Come along.'

# A Visit

OUR walk through the countryside was another revelation to Roger, not alone for its beauty and enchantments, but from the many friendly greetings that we received upon all sides. These latter, in the main, came from folk who were complete 'strangers' to us, and whom the boy thought were part of a wide circle of friends, but we explained that had he been alone, he would have had a similar experience. 'We don't wait for formal introductions here, Roger,' Ruth told him. 'In fact, we don't need them at all.'

We passed much on our way that excited the interest and curiosity of our friend in his new life, a great deal of which I have already recounted to you, until, at length, we reached our destination.

This was a somewhat large dwelling placed amid the most beautiful gardens, with many flower-beds, glistening pools of water, and innumerable trees. The house itself was a square-built edifice with broad windows and a central doorway, but without any marked architectural ornament upon its exterior surface. It seemed to combine, from outward appearance, the dual purposes of a home and a place of work.

The material of which the building was constructed was, I hardly need add, of that pure spirit-world order that veritably lives in its superb tones of colouring, as compared with the heavy dullness of earthly 'bricks and mortar'.

This was the first view at close quarters that Roger had had of anything like a large building, and he could not resist the impulse to pass his hand over the surface of the 'stone'.

'It's real enough, Roger,' said Ruth.

'Yes, but it's warm,' he replied; 'at least, it's not cold !'

We smiled in concert, for every new friend's enthusiasm has something fresh about it, in spite of the fact that we have experienced this same thing over and over again.

By this time our arrival had been perceived, and our host was awaiting us at his front-door. He was an American Indian of handsome and imposing appearance, tall and dignified. He gave us a warm-hearted welcome as we presented Roger to him. We explained that he was but newly arrived, and that we had brought him to these realms, and were now disporting ourselves by acting as his ciceroni.

'And so,' said our host, with a merry laugh, 'you are including me among the sights.'

We hastened to disclaim any such uncomplimentary intention, which only made our friend laugh the more as our explanations seemed to become more involved! At last Ruth said that we had better desist as the patch was rapidly becoming worse than the hole.

It should be mentioned that our host had learned sufficient of our mother-tongue for all practical purposes in connection with his work, and in here setting down his words I have therefore omitted all such slight linguistic 'irregularities' that cause his friends—and admirers—on earth such immense joy, and which, incidentally, equally amuse the speaker of them! Most of our conversation has taken place by the thought process—we are old friends—so that he reveals himself to us as the learned, cultured expert that he is.

In common with the great majority of his race, he has retained his picturesque name, with some slight adaptation to spirit world conditions and circumstances, so that he is known widely in these and other realms of light as Radiant Wing, the first part of that appellation being the adaptation to which I have just referred. It is self-explanatory in that it should—and does here, of course—convey to the onlooker its meaning through the flow of light that leaves the tips of his head-dress.

My friends of earth may wonder why feathered head-dresses should be worn in such a place as the spirit world. The answer is simple: all that is beautiful is preserved, and because some feature, in itself beautiful, appertains to the earth, that is no reason why we should be denied it in these lands. The fact is that we are *not* denied it, nor shall we deny ourselves anything because, or for fear that, folk on earth may disapprove.

If the truth be told, we care not a fig for what the earth people may think of what we do or do not, and we are certainly not going to take orders from such inferior minds, or, indeed, from any kind of mind on earth! No person is forced in these lands to submit to anything of which he disapproves. He is at liberty to seek elsewhere in the avoidance of offence to his fastidious susceptibilities. Equally, he is always at liberty to emerge from his obscurity or seclusion if he eventually feels that he was mistaken. The latter is what always happens!

The head-dress, then, of our host is very fine, displaying a series of rainbow-tints in the most delicate shades. The feathers of which it is constructed have not been taken from a bird. They would have to be taken from a *living* bird, if taken at all—an impossible and revolting supposition—as there are no *dead* birds in the spirit world. The feathers, therefore, are wholly fabricated from spirit-world substance, and fashioned by skilful hands and minds into an absolute verisimilitude of the real article. It should be added that such a head-dress is not worn constantly, but upon the more formal occasions.

We had already explained to Roger that Radiant Wing's principal work was that of a healer to incarnate folk, which he carries on through the agency of an earthly instrument. He is, in addition, a great experimenter, ever searching for new methods in the application of the various resources at his command in many different combinations.

Our host invited us within, and knowing something of my proclivities for gathering information concerning the activities of our life here, he assumed, he said, that we wished to see something of what was going on in his particular department.

We found ourselves in a very pleasant apartment which was, by all appearances, his own particular 'den', and there explained that apart from his actual healing work, he also trained others in the art, mostly young people, many of them, he informed us, just about Roger's age.

He then led us into his 'laboratory', and we were introduced to a number of young men—his students and probationers as he described them.

It was a spacious chamber, upon one side of which were reposing many varieties of flasks, vials, and small jars, each of them containing some substance in a wide range of colours. There were many large diagrams depicting the different parts of the human body, while a number of anatomical models in full colour were displayed in other parts of the room.

'You will understand,' our host explained, 'that it is essential for us to know all about human anatomy and the functions of the body, together with the many ailments that earth people suffer from, before we can even begin to heal them. We are no different in this respect from the doctors on earth. Our methods of treatment, of course, are entirely different. We use materials and forces which the earth doctors do not possess. They belong purely to the spirit world.

'Our methods are very much simpler. For example, look at the glass vessels on those shelves. They contain various ointments for healing an enormous number of complaints. The colours you see have little significance of themselves in the matter of actual healing. They are used to distinguish each unguent, and the especial value of the colour is revealed when we mix one component with another, for as soon as we start blending the colour naturally changes, just as the artist's colours change as he blends his pigments. So you see we are to know at once the precise amount of any one substance that is mixed with another by the tone of blend. In this way we can modify by increasing or diminishing one substance or another according to the particular requirements of the case we are treating.

'For those with an eye for colour these mixtures are a very great pleasure and joy, for our blendings produce an almost unlimited range of beautiful tones.

'Apart from learning the A B C of the healing art, my student friends here also help me to find new blends, and from this we may find a new healing balm for our earth friends in their bodily ailments. What you see on the shelves are merely samples of the spiritual substance. As we attend each case, wherever it may be, our materials are always freshly compounded. By our previous experiments and knowledge, we shall know what colour or blend to use, and so our medicaments are in their right proportions.

'That is but one part of our method of treatment. Another is by light ray, and that we cannot put in flasks and bottles upon our shelves. We *can* show you what happens, though.' He turned to Roger. 'Did you, my son, see from Monsignor's house a large building with a bright blue ray streaming down upon it? You did. That blue ray has a soothing effect upon earth people as well as upon us here. Let me show you. Draw closely round me, my friends.'

We gathered about our host in a small circle. In a moment we perceived a bright blue beam of light descend upon us, and we instantly felt its most soothing effect—not, of course, that we were in *need* of it!

Radiant Wing then had the beam reduced to a small pencil of light, bringing it to focus upon each of our hands in turn.

'You see,' he said, 'we can direct the light on to any area, and in any width we wish, from a broad beam to this small ray. It depends upon the nature of the trouble we are working on.'

It was fascinating to watch him maneuver and manipulate the light wherever he wished it to fall.

'Now here is another kind of ray. Watch.'

The blue beam ceased, and in its place a bright red one descended.

'This,' he explained, 'is a stimulating light; it provides energy: it builds up not only an affected part after treatment, but the whole body, and that is greatly needed on earth at this moment. Our friends of earth need not fear that we shall run short !'

There was a distinct feeling of warmth with the red ray, and Roger remarked upon it.

'That is so, my son. Usually some warmth is needed with the application of the red ray, but we have special heat-rays, where we work with heat alone. The colours of these rays are more for distinguishing purposes, though the colour does help. But the force is really in the ray itself rather than in the colour.

'Well, now, I think you've seen everything, except a demonstration of our work, and that, I'm afraid, we can't show you here. But I must introduce you to my family. Come along into the garden.'

Our host opened a door that led directly into the garden, and we stepped out of doors. Turning to our left, we found ourselves in a most exquisite garden. It was very broad and with two long walls upon either side. Our friend explained that these were not to establish his 'territorial rights', but merely to hide from first sight the grounds that were upon the other sides. In addition they formed a perfect background to the tall plants and flowering shrubs that were growing immediately in front of them.

Equally spaced throughout the length of the walls were fairly wide openings beneath rounded arches, the whole of which produced a most pleasing antique effect. There were many grand trees flourishing in the full vigour of their heavenly growth, free from the winds that deform so many trees on earth, and here displaying their *true* form in unblemished nature.

In the centre of this haven, there was a lily-pond sunk below the level of the ground, with wide steps leading down to a paved surround.

We could see no evidence of the family, but in response to a call from our friend, there came bounding across the large trace of grass upon which we were standing, two beautiful creatures, one a large dog, and the other a puma.

I have omitted to mention that as we emerged from the laboratory, the small bird that Roger had retained in his hand, then flew away in a direct line to a huge tree. He now emerged bringing with him, as it were, a raven and a macaw.

Radiant Wing held out his arms, and the two birds at once perched upon them. The small bird flew back to Roger.

'What do you think of my family?' Radiant Wing asked. 'The dog, the raven and the macaw are my own. The small bird you have there, my son, belongs to friends who are still on earth, and this lovely puma, as well, belongs to one of them, who is also my instrument on earth.'

The colours of the macaw contrasted vividly with the blackness of the raven and the soft grey of the sparrow.

Roger was obviously a trifle timid of the puma, no doubt from his recollection of the same kind of animal on earth, but our host at once reassured him.

'You need have no fear, my son,' said he. 'See, she is without her wildness, and wishes harm to no one.'

Ruth had stooped down and was stroking and playing with the lovely creature, which was as gentle as a lamb.

'She is not the only one of her kind here, by any means,' continued our host, 'but their dispositions are all the same— harmless and gentle. You see, the two chief earthly factors are gone from all the animals in these lands—the need for food, which makes them prey upon others, and fear of both their own creature-kind and of human kind. Remove these two, and there you have the result. They are a great joy to us—and to themselves. Try for yourself, my son.'

Roger bent down beside Ruth, and in a moment had lost his misgivings in stroking the puma's thick fur.

'She is the mad one,' said Radiant Wing, 'and continually keeps all the others "on the stretch". Watch her now with the little bird.'

Roger held up his hand and the sparrow flew into the air only a short distance above the ground, but high enough to be provokingly out of reach of the puma. At this height he flew in a somewhat erratic manner, hither and thither, without appearing to be upon any direct course. The puma immediately gave chase, and as the bird followed a zig-zag way so his companion on the ground tried to emulate him. The acrobatics she was obliged to perform sent us all into roars of laughter, while we could but admire the nimbleness of the agile creature on the ground. The latter made the most astonishing leaps into the air, evidently sure of catching her small friend on the wing, but she was foiled upon every occasion by the bird moving an inch or two higher, or to right or left.

'What would happen,' asked Roger, 'if the puma actually caught up with the bird?'

'Why, nothing,' answered Radiant Wing with a laugh; 'it would be impossible, even if they were not the very best of friends, which, of course, they are. There are no enemies here.'

The game was quickly ended, however, by the bird swooping down upon the puma, and alighting upon the latter's head, who trotted back to us, and rolled herself over on the grass in evident satisfaction with her performance.

Radiant Wing again turned to Roger: 'Now you know where I live, my son, I hope you will visit us whenever you wish. My boys and myself will always be delighted to see you. Or, if you wish, just walk into the garden and enjoy yourself with my family. You may not always find all of them here; sometimes these two', he slightly raised his arms with the two large birds upon them, 'and the dog go with me when I'm on my earth missions. But you know the small bird, and friend puma is most times hereabouts, and ready to play.'

Roger was delighted with this invitation, and thanked our friend warmly, as did Ruth and I, for spending so much time upon us and our new charge.

# Spirit Intercourse

As we strolled along after leaving Radiant Wing, it was easy to see that Roger was fairly deep in thought, no doubt pondering what he had seen both in the house and in the garden of our friend.

At length he spoke. 'What astonishes me, is that all this is unknown to the world. How all this can be going on without somebody knowing about it, is more than I can understand.'

'By the world, you mean the earth, Roger. No, all this is not entirely unknown to the earth people. Some of them are aware of it, but by comparison with the earth's millions only a very few.'

'And how do *they* know?'

'Because they have been told, friend Roger. We have told them. I don't mean Ruth and I, though we have done our microscopic share in the work. But the telling has been going on for years. The earth has never been left high and dry, without someone to tell them about all this. Latterly, the flow of revelation has increased, but you must remember that one of the greatest ecclesiastical establishments on earth has long ago decreed that all revelation ceased when the last of the apostles passed from the earth. Since then—silence. Do you think that sounds at all likely from what you have seen, so far, of the way things are done here?'

'*No*; I do not.'

'Yet, that is the fact. Others believe that to know, or even try to know, anything about the "after-life" is against Holy Writ. So there is another "dead-end". "We are not meant to know. If we were we should *have* been told"—that's what those folk say. Yet they *have* been told—officially; and in the very book that they say is against this knowledge. Strange, isn't it? Those people read that book piously—perhaps too piously—and fail to perceive that it is crammed, literally crammed with psychic lore of every kind. They will swallow whole accounts of it, but because those phenomena still happen, *now*, they will have nothing to do with them. If it was right in those far-off days—and it was—then it must be right now—which it is. Officially, of course there is silence.'

'Wouldn't you think it to be in the interests of any religion to know, or at least to try to find out?'

'Yes, Roger; that's what you would think. The position on earth is roughly this. Of the two principal Churches, one says decisively, dogmatically, that anyone is a fool who denies the existence of psychic phenomena of all kinds, but with equal insistence says that the cause of them is none other than the devil himself, or some of his satellites. That is what Omar meant when he said that there are nice people on earth who would call him—and all the rest of us—just plain devils. Isn't the whole notion too preposterous for words?'

'It is, but can't something be done about it?'

Ruth and I smiled at the healthy, vigorous enthusiasm of our young friend.

'Roger, dear,' said Ruth, 'your feelings do you great credit. We both know exactly how you feel. Monsignor and I had the same experience. We should have liked to have taken people's silly heads and banged them together, and tried to knock some sense into them, but we were restrained—by wiser minds than ours.'

'Now,' I said, 'let me tell you what happened with the other important Church I mentioned. That Church held an inquiry into the whole subject of communication with the earth, ordered by no less a functionary than the Archbishop himself. They investigated very thoroughly and deliberated very carefully, and compiled a report of their findings. The majority were in favour, and declared that communication did in *fact* exist. Splendid. Now, Roger, if you are fond of a joke —we know you are—get ready to laugh loudly: *the whole report was officially suppressed.*

'Peculiar, isn't it, how people do not want to know about us and the life we are living here? Of course there are very naughty people who say that if that report had been against us, it would have been published with a flourish of trumpets to help it on. I haven't told you the actual sequel yet. The Archbishop who ordered the inquiry and then ordered the report to be suppressed, has since come to live here himself.

'It's a difficult job, my Roger, to try to undo some things we wish we had never done. That good prelate has all my sympathy, for I too left behind me things which I had rather left undone. By great good fortune I have been enabled to put them right; not entirely right, you must understand, but suffi-ciently so to make very little difference. And where I spoke with vigour when I was on earth, I have since spoken with extra double-strength vigour to make up for it. I can feel now in my mind a great calm and contentment that were lacking before. When we get home I will show you a volume that was the cause of the earthly trouble many years ago. It was terrible stuff!'

Ruth laughed. 'Don't get overheated, my dear,' she said, 'there are much worse things on earth than that old book—*and* more foolish!'

'Both those Churches take a peculiar interest in this world—a *religious* interest, of course. Neither knows what precisely to expect in the way of an after-life. An after-life there must be, naturally, but they can suggest nothing that does not imply some description of an essentially *religious* life. In effect, it means that the earth life is the *real* material life, and that the after-life is conducted upon holy lines of some sort. Certainly the whole atmosphere will be pious, and totally unlike what man has been accustomed to on earth. They are right in the latter; this life is totally unlike the earth life, but not in the way they mean.

'What's to be the end of it all, then? Will the Churches eventually find the truth? That is a large question. As they are at present constituted, nothing could be done. They are perfectly contented as they are. The first of the two I mentioned claims to be the one true Church, and infallible. There would not seem to be much hope there. The second Church possesses no authority whatever. Within broad limits—very broad ones—its members can think and believe what they like. The bishops have little or no authority over their clergy in matters of "faith". There are some ministers who wholeheartedly support the spirit world as it really is, because they have spiritual knowledge derived directly from us. Even if this particular Church pronounced in our favour officially, it by no means follows that the clergy and the laity would do the same thing. There are some who have this knowledge, and uphold the Church as well—with all its strange doctrines. In that they are trying to face both ways at once. But when they come here, they must eventually face only one way.

'You can see, Roger, what difficulties are in the way when it comes to official acknowledgment of the true manner of life in the spirit world. That is why the truth is in the hands of unofficial folk. You see what a lecture your simple proposition has brought upon you!'

Ruth suggested that we sit down for a while. We found a spot beneath a tree upon slightly rising ground, where we could see in the distance a glittering expanse of water.

'Doesn't it seem an awful pity, Roger,' said Ruth, 'that so many millions of people on earth should know nothing about this lovely land? And doesn't it seem outrageous that officially they should be "warned off" from knowing anything, and for the most silly, stupid reasons? What harm, what possible harm could there be in knowing all about us and the life we live? One would think we are absolute outcasts, or peculiar people it were better not to have anything to do with. It makes me furious.'

'Now, don't you get overheated, my dear,' I said. 'This wholesale ignorance isn't a new thing. It's been going on for hundreds of years. That's the real trouble. It's been going on too long, so that people have got into the one way of thinking—mostly the religious or theological way. You know, Roger, it's not so very surprising that hundreds of people, when they arrive here and find out the truth, go about like a "mighty wind", and want to go back to earth to shout the truth at last to the folk they've left behind them. Some of them actually do go back, but the result is dismal—on both sides. Their voices cannot be heard—that is, heard in the very place where they want them to be.

'Take yourself, my boy. Ruth and I could lead you to a little spot on earth where we could make ourselves known among old friends. We could introduce you to them, and ask if they would convey a message for you to your people at your old home. Very well. What would happen next? Remember your relations would be complete strangers to our friends, and presumably your people know nothing about communication between the two worlds, or if they know, do not believe it can be done. What do you suppose would be the result when our friends presented themselves at your parents' house, and said the had a message from their Roger? You know best what would happen, because you know them. As a matter of interest, Roger, what *would* happen?'

The boy thought a moment. 'They would be civil, at least,' he said, 'but a bit grim. Probably think your friends cranks, if not altogether mad.'

'They don't *look* like cranks, Roger; so they might be able to escape that. But mad—yes, perhaps; though they don't give any evident or unmistakable signs of that either. What next?'

'They might think it in shockingly bad taste.'

'Ah, that would be difficult to overcome. Bad taste that our friends should intrude upon their bereavement, and so on. Then what?'

'I rather fancy your friends would be shown the front door. After that, they would discuss it between themselves, and go off to see their vicar. He would listen civilly, and tell them he *had* heard about such things, but that they were far better left alone.'

'That's about it, Roger. The same old story all over again, and one we have to recount, and keep on recounting, to people as they arrive here in their thousands, and want to go back to earth to speak.

'The chief trouble with the Churches is that they cannot make the truth about this world fit in with their theology.

They don't realize that they are going about things the wrong way: they must make their theology fit the truth, and that means a wholesale clearance of everything that does not accord with it. At present they prefer the shadow to the substance; they prefer creeds and doctrines and dogmas. They are not realists—far from it.

'Let us put the matter plainly, even crudely, if you wish it. Here are three of us human beings who once lived on earth. We have passed through the experience of dying, and now we are seated in the spirit world upon some delightfully soft turf beneath a beautiful tree, with all the lovely countryside round about us, and reaching for miles away into the distance. It is all unquestionably real and solid. It is no "spiritual experience" in the religious sense, but an "everyday" experience of a very ordinary nature. We are here—all three of us—because, by virtue of man's spiritual heritage, it is our right to be here, and *not* because of what we believed on earth, or through the merits of any particular Church to which we belonged. Ruth will tell you herself that she gave up going to church altogether. Yet she is here with us, and she will tell you she was an awful heathen in the eyes of her Church. Another Church would call her a heretic and a schismatic, and doomed to who-knows-what terrible place for her sins.

'As for myself, I was a priest of the Church, and should have known better—but didn't. You, Roger, are young, but I believe you did not become exactly a pillar of your Church. Now between us, and strictly from the theological point of view, you two should not be here at all, if this place is reserved for folk like me. If my theology, and all the doctrines and dogmas I rigorously upheld and preached about, have brought me to this particular region of the spirit world, then you two have no business to be here at all. You can't say, theologically speaking, that either of you is the least fitted to be in my company, for you, Ruth, on your own terrible confession, were no church-goer at all latterly in your earth life, and you, Roger, were only half-hearted in it. It's extremely difficult for me to adjudicate between you, and settle who is the worse sinner. You're both pretty bad, it would seem, and I have no business to be in your company, or you have no business to be in mine. But the stubborn fact is that you *are* here, and so am I.

'What is the, conclusion? There's only one: that something is wrong somewhere with all the theology. The theology doesn't fit the facts.

'Let's go further. When you were on earth, Roger, did you go about your daily life in a "pious" frame of mind—it sounds a silly question to ask, but did you?'

'No, Monsignor; I certainly did not.'

'Of course, you didn't; no rationally constituted person does. One may have pleasant thoughts, kindly thoughts, and do pleasant, kindly actions, but that is not going about and behaving in a "pious" manner, and generally being sanctimonious and altogether objectionable. Now, how do you feel about things at this present moment? Any different?'

'Not a particle.'

'And so, if a bulletin were issued it might read like this: "no change has been reported in Roger's condition other than his now feeling *perfectly* fit in bodily health. He is in the most cheerful spirits (as well as being with them), and is at this moment thoroughly enjoying himself—if his face is any indication of the state of his mind. He is pleased to inform all theologians that he does not feel the least particle 'pious' or 'holy', and is most thankful that he feels himself, and nobody else". Would you subscribe to that declaration, my lad?'

'I would, indeed, Monsignor. I wouldn't swap this back for the old earth.'

'*Exchange*, Roger, *exchange*. You must understand that "swap" is a word that would never be used by a disembodied entity; that you would be expected to speak the most perfect language, entirely free from all slang and vulgarisms, and that everything you say must be profound in nature and weighty in substance. That's how we are expected to behave by most of the earth people—the uninstructed ones. Now the great point is that there are no evident signs of piety or holiness, or even of religiosity to be seen here, nor do we go about quoting scripture or other uplifting texts to one another, and behaving in a thoroughly unnatural manner.

'In brief: we are not living in a religious institution or a religious world as a whole, but in a sane, sensible world, of incomparable beauty, where we can work and play, as we wish, and laugh to our heart's content, and where, moreover—and this is vitally important—*where we can be ourselves*, and not be as others on earth would mistakenly have us to be.

'Isn't it odd that when I had plenty of pulpits at my disposal to preach from, I had nothing much to say—as I see it now? And now I *have* a great deal to say, I have no pulpit.'

# Spirit Locomotion

WE HAD been walking along in leisurely fashion when
Roger turned to me: 'Is walking the only means of getting
about?' he asked. 'I can't see any roads anywhere, and the
countryside seems to stretch for miles.'

'It does stretch for miles,' I replied; 'thousands of them.
What you mean, Roger, is: where's the transport system and
what is it? The answer is that we each of us carry our own
:system about with us, the most efficient and the most rapid in
the universe. That is in addition to walking. So far we have
relied upon our two legs since we brought you here, but the
time has obviously come when we must show you something
of what we can really do here.

'Personal locomotion is done by the thought process, and
it's perfectly easy to do when once you're shown how; then it
becomes second nature. It may sound like a contradiction in

terms, but the thought process of locomotion hardly requires thinking about when once you're accustomed to it.

'Can you remember when you first learned to walk on earth, Roger?'

'No, I can't say I do.'

'I don't suppose there are many who can. But there did come a time when you could keep upright successfully and without tumbling down. Since then you have walked many miles on earth, and some distance here as well. Do you ever think about it?

'Suppose you are sitting in a chair and you wish to rise and cross the room, you simply rise and walk without thinking of all the muscles that have to be controlled to get your limbs on the move. You do all that without thinking, though there must be some thought somewhere, obviously, or else you would remain rooted where you were. What particular line does the thought take: that you must walk, or that you wish to rise, or that you want to cross the room, or all three? It doesn't matter. Basically, the desire is to get across the room—the other side of the room is your destination. And that's all you need to consider here in using the thought process to move yourself about.

'At first, you must make a really conscious effort; you must think about it. A little practice, and you'll find that no sooner do you think, than you are wherever you wish to be. Sounds rather fantastic, don't you think?'

'It does a bit.'

'It's the sort of thing sceptical folk on earth like to poke fun at, and generally ridicule. Such a splendid joke, and causes roars of laughter. The same folk should take out their Bibles and study them a little more, and then bring their wits to bear upon what they read there.

'A great many of our ways here form a constant source for derision among the incarnate, Roger. Taking the earth as the standard for everything, including life itself, they cannot imagine anything better or different. Of course, they'll regard "heaven" as a place or condition of perfection, but of perfection of what, they know not, and cannot imagine. I would say seriously to such people not to pour scorn upon *our* spirit lands and the way we do things unless they are prepared to provide better. If there is any single feature or factor or law to which they take exception, let them at once suggest a better or finer or more sensible way, and all of us here in the spirit world will gladly listen and see that their suggestions reach the right quarter.

'We need not, of course, worry ourselves unduly about these folk. If there is anything of which they disapprove when they come here, they are at liberty to depart, to remove themselves, leaving us in the enjoyment of our own mode of life, while they betake themselves elsewhere and create their own bleak void—and live in it.'

My two companions had such a merry twinkle in their eyes, that I subsided into laughter.

'You know, Roger,' said Ruth, 'Monsignor feels very strongly on some subjects. He caught the public eye and ear when he was a priest, and since coming here he has done the same thing again in a very different way. He knows how hard it is to get people to shake off old and wrong beliefs for the truth, and it really vexes him. That is perhaps one of the penalties, if one can call it so, for being in such close touch with the earth. I'm not, though I visit it occasionally with Monsignor purely to watch proceedings and give a greeting to our friends there.

'Thoughts are very real, Roger,' she continued, 'and can reach us here from earth as easily and as surely as they can

reach us here between ourselves. And ours can go to the earth
people too, though they don't always notice them.'

'Perhaps that's what accounts for the feeling I've had. I
don't know how to describe it, but there seems to be a sort of
pulling, if you follow; a kind of urge to go—well—I don't
know where. Oh, this is all terribly vague. I've felt peculiar;
not ill, but restless, I suppose.'

'Poor Roger,' said Ruth; 'I think we can diagnose your
"complaint" without difficulty. The trouble is caused by
friends or relations, or both perhaps, sending out a few
thoughts of grief. It's natural they should be sorry you've left
them, though their sorrow is not deep, or else you would have
felt it very keenly yourself, and that would have been trouble-
some. I doubt if this feeling will get stronger, but if it should,
tell us, Roger, and we'll help to dispel it. You have no
personal regrets yourself on any account?'

'None whatever, Ruth, thank you.'

'Good; that's a great help.'

'We seem to have wandered a trifle from Roger's question. Do you recall, Ruth, soon after we had arrived here,
how we discussed the quaint notion of "angelic beings"
having wings? Strange idea, isn't it, Roger. The only thing
one can imagine is that long ago, people, especially artists,
must have wondered how "angelic beings" managed to get
about. Legs would seem preposterous, out of the question,
by being far too mundane. I mean for perambulating purposes. But if one eliminates the use of legs, what remains?
Nothing, so far as I can see, and I suppose that is how it struck
the artists.

'Angels must be able to move; they can't be rooted to one
spot for all eternity. That, one supposes, led some genius to
invent huge wings for all inhabitants of the spirit world. I
believe Satan himself was endowed with a pair, as, of course,

it was essential for *him* to be extremely mobile so that he could get about comfortably and quickly "seeking the ruin of souls", as one pretty prayer expresses it.

'Can you think of anything more clumsy and ponderous than having an enormous pair of wings fastened upon you somewhere in the region of the shoulder-blades? I can't.'

'I should imagine,' said Roger, 'that a large flock of angels would stir up an awful breeze when in flight.'

'Roger, I'm afraid you're being highly irreverent in refer-ring, to a large number of angels as a flock.'

'Well, what would they be, then?'

'I really don't know; it's not easy to find a word for what doesn't exist, except poetically, perhaps. But you are severely practical when you say that a great concourse—that is more elegant than flock, Roger—would disturb the atmospheric conditions, and that's something the artist fellows never thought of. It is astonishing how the idea originally caught on and has persisted even to the present day. The conventional way of portraying a being from this world—and they still don't look upon us as human; only half-human—is with two large wings. Even symbolically it's a pretty poor idea. As a means of personal locomotion, wings would be useless, an impossibil-ity, and we should be anatomical monstrosities. We're obvi-ously not built for such apparatus, the wonders and marvels of the spirit world notwithstanding.

'Angels with their fantastic wings being another of the many extraordinary misconceptions of the true way of things in spirit lands, it really is no wonder that in the end, with all these falsifications, the people of earth regard us as sub-human. The higher we go in spiritual advancement the less human we become, it would seem, and the more grim. Did either of you ever see a picture of an angel, or a piece of sculpture of one, especially in a cemetery, where the artist had put a smile upon the face of his subject? Smiling is not "heavenly" enough. Isn't it too awful for words? Aren't you very glad, Roger, that things are as they are, and *not* as they might be if some folk were given a free hand?'

'I should jolly well think so,' the boy agreed.

'A loud *Amen* to that, ' exclaimed Ruth.

'Otherwise,' I added, 'we should have to get all the doors heightened to allow sufficient clearance for our wings. Truth is better than fiction, in this case, Roger, and the truth of moving ourselves about these lands by the process of applied thought is the simplest and best. Now suppose you try.'

'What do I have to do?'

'Only a little thinking. You needn't be alarmed. Everyone has to try at some time. Ruth and I were delighted with the results when we first managed, and you will be the same.'

We were sitting on the grass at the time, and I suggested that Roger desire himself to be at a tree we could see, some quarter-mile distant.

'You need not make a gigantic effort of will, old man,' I said; 'merely think firmly that you would like to be under that tree yonder—or anywhere else you fancy. I suggest the tree because it's not too far off, and you can see us easily from there. As "a good outset is half the voyage", Ruth and I will send a thought with you. Now, then; off you go.'

Of course, he vanished from our presence, as we knew he would, and we saw him beneath the distant tree, where he waved to us. We waved back, and then joined him.

'Well, did you enjoy the journey, Roger?' asked Ruth.

The boy laughed. 'There was nothing much to enjoy; one second I was there, the next here. But it *is* wonderful though; there's no getting away from that. What a marvellous feeling of independence it gives you. Wouldn't I love to have been able to do this back on earth. My goodness, it would have frightened the life out of mother, though.'

'Yes, it has its possibilities on earth, and its impossibilities. There it would revolutionize life. Here it is part of life, and has been, ever since there's been a spirit world.'

'Here is something that occurs to me,' said Roger. 'Would it be possible for me to lose myself. I mean, suppose I got out of touch with either you or Ruth; what then?'

'You mean,' I replied, 'suppose Ruth or I were to take you to some spot far away from this particular locality, and then disappear and leave you to your own devices?'

'Yes, that's it.'

'Then your own devices would get you out of your difficulty very nicely, Roger. Don't be disturbed, though. We shouldn't dream of abandoning you on a door-step, so to speak, and you for someone else to find!

'This is precisely what would happen. Suppose for a moment you could not conjure up in your mind any sort of recollection of our house, there is yet the connecting link between ourselves—the three of us. And if the worst really came to such extremes, you would have but to concentrate your mind upon either Ruth or myself, and you would see and feel an instantaneous response. So that, wherever we happened to be, you could come to us. I say you *could* come to us, but it by no means follows that you would, because we might prevent you—or send someone to do so. You see, my boy, Ruth and I penetrate into some very unpleasant quarters of the spirit world, places that we have not mentioned to you yet, and it would not do for you to approach them.

'Wherever Ruth and I might be, you would always be in touch with us in mind. Of course, you have not forgotten our house, its arrangements, and surroundings, so really the matter doesn't arise. Merely for the sake of argument, if you did forget there's Radiant Wing's home and his delightful family. You could hardly fail to recollect all that we saw there, and so you would have that refuge in case of failure of memory, and *he* would look after you.

'But there's one thing to be considered, though perhaps we have not mentioned it specifically, and that is the impossibility of memory failure. That resolves your difficulty finally and completely. You've *not* forgotten our home and all its appurtenances, have you?'

'No, indeed not; it's all very clear in my mind.'

'Exactly; and so it will remain. You cannot forget, because the memory is itself unfailing in operation. I know one can imagine all kinds of difficulties or perplexities of the same sort, but they have no substance, and cannot be otherwise. To lose one's self, for instance: impossible. To forget something or other: equally impossible.

'You spoke about a transport system, Roger, no doubt having in mind the usual earthly services and arrangements: trains, buses, cars and so on. As you see, we don't need any of those for carrying us about these lands.'

'Yes, but suppose you want to move house. How do you shift the stuff?'

'Why, we shouldn't find much difficulty, no difficulty, in fact, in moving it. We may not be giants here, Roger, but we do have powers—and we use them when called upon to do so. We could, between us, move all the furniture in our house with the greatest ease, and feel none the worse for it afterwards. We shouldn't have blisters on our hands, nor strained backs! We could transport the whole contents of our home a dozen times over, while the earth folk were thinking about it—and without fuss and breakages!

'We do move house when we feel we should like to live in another part of these realms. We are not necessarily tied to one spot, or unable to move without many formalities. The fact is, once we have chosen a spot in which to have our dwelling we mostly stay there, at least until such time as we leave the realm altogether. But we don't become stale, as it were, or tired of our surroundings, for the reason that there are always changes of some sort going on, large or small, to alter or enhance the precincts of our dwellings. For instance, our house, as you see it at this moment, is not exactly as it was when I first arrived. With our various activities we thought we should like to enlarge it for convenience sake, and so we had an annex built, the fairly large apartment we showed you, with the tapestries on the walls, the long table with the chairs round it, something in the style of the "great hall" in the ancient mansions on earth—and in the spirit world, too. That was one alteration.

'The gardens themselves have undergone all manner of rearranging. That in itself is a delightful occupation carried out by real artists in horticulture and garden design. So you see, the movement of our goods and chattels presents no problem. We don't require great lorries and vans. The mere effort of one person can move the largest piece of furniture, because all things, everything, in this world is endowed with life. There's no such thing as inert matter, as I told you. Between us we could remove the entire contents of our house—or any other house—without the least trouble.

'Now, Roger, would you care to go and see the city at first hand? You've only seen it from the house so far. Come along. Walk—or otherwise? Otherwise, then, by all means.'

# The City

'No one seems to be in a hurry,' observed Roger. 'That's because no one is in a hurry.'

'Oh, of course; that never occurred to me!'

'Just so.'

'If there's any need to hurry, one can be "there" as quick as thought. If there's no need, there's no hurry.'

We had reached the environs of the city, and we were on ground sufficiently elevated to give the boy a capital introduction to the 'metropolis' in one comprehensive view. From where we stood he could see the many stately buildings, each with its surrounding gardens and miniature lakes, radiating, as with the spokes of a wheel, from a grand central building. He remarked that there were no roads as such, but instead were broad thoroughfares *paved* with superb grass.

Upon the dome of the central building he perceived a brilliant shaft of pure light descending, and inquired what it was.

'That domed building, Roger,' we told him, 'is where we meet upon the more formal occasions to welcome the great personages from the higher realms. It is not precisely a temple, though one might call it that for want of a better name. Nor is it specifically a place of worship, as it would be regarded on earth. We hold no services there. When we forgather there to meet these great visitants, the whole assembly is never very long. Their visits are brief as a rule, though naturally we are seated comfortably a little while before they arrive, and remain a little while after their departure. But brief as the whole proceedings are, all that is necessary is accomplished within that short space. No time is wasted upon "non-essentials" or upon useless formularies! The bright beam you see descending upon the dome is permanently there.'

'It must be an immensely strong light to be able to see it in this broad daylight.'

'It is a strong light, have no doubt about it, and considering the source whence it comes, that's not surprising. It comes from the greatest Source of all, my Roger. Yet the light itself is not blinding, is it?'

'When we first talked to you about a city, you hardly expected anything like this, did you, Roger?' asked Ruth, 'though that's rather a silly question,' she added, 'because you didn't expect anything in particular—like so many people.'

'I don't know what I really expected. I suppose I had something in mind comparable with an earth city.'

'The secret is that we are much simpler here than the earth ever can ever be—unless the earth radically alters its general mode of life. Bethink you, Roger, of the myriads of things we don't need here. In an idle moment you could compile such a list of commodities that are not required for life in the spirit as world reach the dimensions of a stores' catalogue!

'Think, now. Start with the domestic arrangements of a house. Food, for instance. We don't need food, so that means the elimination of a huge industry comprising all the various departments of eating and drinking, and all the vessels and utensils for manufacturing it, cooking it, and serving it.

'Our clothes are provided for us by the operation of a natural law—another vast industry dispensed with.

'The transport system you have already seen here!'

'Conspicuous by its absence.'

'Very much so.'

'Then think of all the trades and professions that have no counterpart or equivalent in these lands.'

'Undertakers, for instance,' suggested Roger with a laugh.

'Or politicians,' added Ruth.

'Don't forget priests and parsons—even bishops,' I said. 'Perhaps it would be as well not to be too specific. The undertakers are more pleasantly employed here, and the politicians more usefully!'

'As you can see, Roger, of shops there are none,' Ruth pointed out, 'because there is no commerce of any kind.'

'Then what do you do when you want something?'

'Such as——?'

'Well——' He reflected a moment. 'I don't seem able to think of anything,' he finished, with more surprise to himself than to Ruth and me. We laughed.

'That's rather odd, isn't it Roger? You don't seem to want anything. Those clothes you are wearing are the clothes you arrived with here. By the way, whenever you feel you would like to change to your spirit clothes proper, you can do so at once. As you are attired now, everyone knows you for a new arrival. If you wish to appear as a "seasoned resident", the same as Ruth and I, you'll have to put off the old and put

on the new.   So there, at least, is something you would
want—spirit clothes to make the change.'

'If there are no shops or tailors, what's to be done?'

'Nothing, or at least very little.  You would like to discard
the old style of attire, Roger?'

'I should very much.'

'Then do so, my dear boy.'

'Yes, but *how*?'

'I'm afraid we can't tell you *how* it happens, but look at
yourself, Roger.  Your eyes have been on the view before you.
Now glance a little nearer.'

The boy did so, and was astonished to discover that his
old earthly habiliments had given place to bright spirit clothing, full and free, and in absolute keeping with the surroundings.  Ruth and I did the same, and for the first time Roger saw
us in spirit attire.

'Now you can see, Roger, how we should have appeared
in your bedroom had we not returned to our former earth
clothing.  It *might* have frightened you.'

'I'm sure of it,' he said.  He raised a fold of his garments,
and examined it closely, and remarked that it did not seem to
have been made by human hands.

'No, Roger; no hands were employed upon the creating of
these garments, but Ruth and I must tell you, honestly, that we
do not know what natural process comes into operation in the
making of them.  There are many things we must know first,
and so we take things as we find them.  Did you, when you
were on earth, try to analyze every mortal thing that came
your way in life, and try to discover how it was made, and a
hundred other reasons or causes for its existence?  I'm sure
you did not; neither did Ruth nor I.  There's no reason why we
should carry out minute investigations here into the existence

of the many things that are part of our very life. It's problematical if we should be any the better for knowing.

'Our spirit garments are in a class by themselves, though. Do you see that large building a little to the right of us? That's called the hall of fabrics. In there you can inspect thousands of the most wonderful materials and cloths, some of them representing the fabrics that were upon earth—all parts of the earth—during the course of hundreds of years. Others are types of material peculiar to the spirit world alone, both in design and in texture.

'You saw the tapestries hanging on the walls of our home. They were made by Ruth herself in the hall of fabrics. When we were first shown over that hall, Ruth saw numbers of happy folk weaving tapestries, and was immediately taken with the same idea. Since then she has become expert in the art, as you saw at home.'

'It was nothing,' said Ruth; 'you could do the same, Roger, if you had a mind that way. That's one of the principal functions of these places, to teach you to do all manner of things expertly.'

'The hall of fabrics cannot supply you with spirit clothing, Roger,' I said.

'It makes me feel terribly ignorant to see all these halls stuffed with knowledge.'

'Then don't let it, my dear boy. After all, one can experience much the same emotion standing in the presence of a couple of dozen volumes of an encyclopedia, if it comes to that. We are not born with a vast deal of knowledge all ready to hand, as it were. Ruth and I felt the same way about it when *we* were shown all these wonders of knowledge; and so does everyone else. We're all in the same boat, Roger, so we can all be nicely ignorant together!'

'I must say the people don't seem upset about it.'

'These halls of learning are mostly devoted to what on earth are called the arts,' I explained; 'by which I mean painting, music, literature, and so on. Great stress is laid upon those. There are, of course, many others. On earth the arts are regarded more as adjuncts to life than necessities. They could be dispensed with, though the earth would then be more drab than it is already. Here they are vital and are given a wide field. To begin with, without all those industries that we tried to enumerate just now, there is a corresponding freedom for other and far pleasanter occupations.

'There's one thing, Roger, that you won't see here among the arts: and that is musical monstrosities or art abominations masquerading as masterpieces. They have not been thrown out—they were never admitted, and never will be. No shams here, my Roger. "Abandon all pretence ye who enter".'

'What does a person have to do to get taken on in one of these halls, Monsignor?'

'Why, walk through the front entrance, and you'll be left in no doubt. You'll be welcomed with the greatest warmth, and set upon the path of studying whatever it is that has taken your fancy. That's how Ruth began, almost, with her tapestry weaving. She asked could she join the others and be taught the art, and forthwith, without *any* formalities whatever, she did so.'

'And was never so happy in my life,' put in Ruth. 'Charming people, patient and kind, especially if you are "all fingers and thumbs", as I was when I began. Monsignor has spent an enormous amount of time browsing among the books in the principal library. That's a terrible place once you are interested in it. There are millions of books there upon every subject under the sun. Have you ever tried to look up something in an encyclopedia, Roger, especially one that has good illustrations?'

'Yes, rather; a hopeless business, there's so much dallying on the way.'

'Then you can imagine what it's like there in the library. If Monsignor were ever reported missing in these regions, that is the first place where a search party would call.'

'Let us go closer and inspect some of these buildings,' I suggested.

'Are we allowed to go in as we like?'

'Exactly as we like, Roger. No permits required, no opening and closing times, as they are open all day—and that's not difficult as we have no night !'

'Are the same people on duty all the time, then?'

'Oh, dear, no; that would sound like eternal work instead of "eternal rest". You could say truthfully that the work is eternal, but the same people are not employed upon it in an eternal succession without personal remission. We have no division of night and day, but the work is carefully divided among the staffs so that they can have their periods of change and recreation, and everybody is perfectly satisfied.'

Roger remarked that the buildings were of no very great height as judged by the usual earthly standards.

'Well, no; two stories of moderate height are sufficient here, as there are no problems of space limitations. We don't have to build upwards; we have unlimited room to spread ourselves, and the result, you must confess, is excellent.'

Roger expressed his unbounded delight with the beauty and charm of the whole creation with its broad thoroughfares of superb grass, the many flower-beds and trees, the pools of crystal-clear water that provided an exquisite setting for the many fine edifices that comprised the city itself.

'Doesn't it strike you as odd, Roger, that all this beauty, this superlative beauty, should be rather sneered at by so many of the uninstructed on earth? Doesn't the earth recede into something like dingy insignificance beside all this splendour? Yet earth folk, a great many of them, regard *their* world as *the* world, by which all is judged, assessed, or appraised. The smoky, dirty cities and towns of the earth are made the criterion, and this lovely city is treated by them with something that seems remarkably like contempt, if not ridicule.'

Ruth and I between us pointed out the purposes to which the various halls were devoted, and at length Roger expressed his desire to investigate the interior of the hall of engineering, which also included chemical research. We passed in, and were greeted by the man who is 'in charge' of the myriad activities that are in constant performance.

'Why, Monsignor,' said he, 'and Ruth, too. This is a pleasure; we've not seen you for a long time. What can I do for you?'

I explained our errand, and presented Roger to him.

'Of course you've come to the right place, my dear friend.'

We smiled at this little pleasantry, as it has become almost a tradition that the man in charge of each of these great halls will, in similar circumstances, say precisely the same thing—a justifiable pride!

Perhaps of all the halls of learning, this, of engineering and chemistry, concerns the earth most closely, since it is here that so many of the earthly engineering and chemical discoveries have their origin. Many new substances are invented in the spirit world that are subsequently transmitted to people on earth for the benefit of all.

As we passed from room to room we could see chemists and their assistants experimenting with a variety of substances which in time will, when combined, form an entirely new product exactly fitted for its purpose. We were shown how, by synthesis, exact replicas of earthly materials were compounded, since it would be of no use whatever to invent a new substance of purely spirit materials which would not—could not—have any application to earthly uses. The scientist on earth must use earthly materials, and the spirit world scientist must therefore work in a precise counterpart.

It so often happens, our guide told us, that a mere hint to an earthly scientist is enough to set him upon the track of a dozen or more other discoveries. All that the scientists here are concerned with is the initial discovery, and in most cases the rest will follow.

Here also were new substances to be used as building materials for houses or large edifices, and for many other types of building construction. New compounds were in process of being made that would eventually be converted into fabrics of all kinds, light and heavy, for personal clothing, for example, or for upholsteries in houses and homes.

In the mechanical sections old principles were being applied in new directions, to result in better and safer and more commodious means of transport, with greater comfort.

Many inventions we saw, of all kinds, from some simple device for use in the home, to the large machine to be used in one industrial process or another.

Life on earth has become far too complex, and people are spending far too much time in purely material pursuits, usually to the exclusion of the spiritual. Life on earth, therefore, must in the end become simpler, and in doing so will become more enjoyable. The spirit world has much to send to the earth to achieve this end. But the earth world has first to put itself in good order. What is of major importance, the people of earth must learn to banish war from off its face, must learn not to turn to evil purposes that which was transmitted to it for peaceful purposes. In the latter lies disaster; in the former lies happiness.

It is for man himself to choose.

# We Visit the 'Church'

WE HAD left the city and were walking along the edge of a wood when Roger, pointing into the distance said: 'That looks remarkably like a church.'

'It is a church,' said Ruth, 'but with a difference.'

'Would you care to go to inspect it?' I asked, and Roger answering in the affirmative, we turned in that direction.

The 'church' in question had all the appearance of its familiar country counterpart on earth, excepting, of course, that of age. It had antiquity of form without showing the effects of the ravages of time, and there was now no occasion for us to tell the boy that physical decay, brought about by the elements and the passage of years, was a condition that did not exist in the spirit world, and though an edifice might look as though it had been erected but yesterday, it may have been standing many hundreds of years.

The 'church' we were now visiting was no exception to the rule. In point of fact, I do not believe that, in the spirit world, there are any exceptions that are supposed to prove a rule! There were, however, other features about this 'church' that Roger might have passed without realizing their full implication, and so, as we drew close to it, we asked him if he saw anything unusual about it.

The lad had a very keen eye and was quick to seize upon the principal characteristic. 'Yes,' he observed; 'the "church" has a familiar look about it, but its surroundings are so unusual that it almost makes the "church" itself look different.'

'Good for you, Roger,' I said. 'You've only recently come from the earth, and so earthly things are still fresh in your mind, as it were. You can make comparisons with greater fineness.

'The "church" you see here is a complete exemplification of what could be done on earth, if an effort were only to be made, in making the churches there things of real beauty in their externals. The whole of this has been built, including the fabric itself, to show exactly what can be done even in a limited space. As you can see, the territory round the building is spacious, but nevertheless, it has not been used to its full extent, so as to preserve, as nearly as possible, the customary conditions on earth, where space is usually somewhat limited.'

As we drew near we could see a low brick wall running irregularly round the church grounds in imitation of an earthly situation where other land rights encroached. The wall was trim and neat without being too plain and uninteresting. We passed through a lychgate, walking on a wide path that had been made of composite substance to give the appearance of asphalt, for in a matter of pure utility, a grass path would have soon worn 'threadbare' under the tread of many feet, and our reproduction had to be exact.

Flowers being in constant bloom in these lands, we had perforce to strike a compromise between what would be a general appearance in summer and that in winter. To do this many evergreen trees and bushes were introduced, and the flowers were so planted that horticultural anachronisms were avoided as far as each bed was concerned. Some flower-beds were left empty to suggest the extreme of winter when few, if any, flowering things are possible out of doors.

Running along one side of the grounds was a small brook carefully confined to a straight course, and which had its source in a small cascade, while the sides of the brook itself were lined with flowers. Here and there were lily-ponds, while the whole was encircled with many fine trees. In imagination, therefore, one could see the great possibilities of such an arrangement on earth, making full allowance for the infinitely greater beauty of a spirit-world counterpart. Such a scheme and its fulfillment are here, and could be emulated upon earth with the removal of the unsightly and unnecessary burial grounds so often to be seen about church buildings, and so often nothing but a wilderness of weeds and neglect.

Roger noticed at once the absence of a burial-ground, to which so much importance is attached on earth, nor could he see anything in the way of a notice-board.

'Ruth told you there was a difference, you remember, Roger. There are differences within, as well as without. In truth, this is only a church in name and appearance; a sample of what *could* be done if earth folk had a mind to bring about a few alterations. It is only the outside, the surroundings, that we are offering as an example, for this is not a "place of worship" in the earthly sense. In other words, there are no services held here, though what takes place inside is really of more value than what goes on perennially in so many of the earthly churches. Still, we won't pursue that line of thought .... Let us go inside.'

We found the building empty of people when we entered. It was a fair-sized structure built on the lines of a 'parish church', and as it was no church in the strict meaning of the word, there was much absent that would otherwise have been conspicuous: the font, for example, and the pulpit. But what struck Roger most forcibly was the absence of a high altar.

The sanctuary itself remained the same, with the usual flights of steps leading up in a series of 'orders', to the highest, where there was a broad space upon which were a number of handsome chairs, the chief of which, placed in the centre, being slightly more ornate than its fellows. Above them was a fine lancet window, containing some exquisite coloured glass. Instead of the familiar religious pictures, the glass represented pleasant rustic scenes such as one sees depicted in tapestries and the like.

On the wall immediately above the chairs were two inscriptions worked in mosaic, and placed side by side. Roger's attention was immediately attracted to these, and turning to me asked, 'why are those two beams of light coming down on the texts?'

'They're not coming down, Roger; they're *going up and out*.'

The lad read the Latin inscription aloud: '*Gloria in excelsis Deo, et in tefra pax horninibus bonae voluntatis.*'

'Correct, Roger, but if you will forgive me, your pronunciation of the Latin is appalling!'

'That was the way I was taught,' he laughed.

'Of course you were, my dear fellow. So was I, at first. That's another example of the cult of the hideous on earth, the rule being: if possible always choose the ugly!'

'Oh, come, Monsignor; things aren't altogether as bad as that.'

'Not far from it, then.   You know what those words mean—if not, they've been conveniently translated for you: "Glory to God in the highest, and on earth peace to *men of good will*." Note the last, Roger.   Different from what you were used to, perhaps, on earth.   It's the better rendering, because it means so much more.   Peace, my dear boy, will never come to the folk of earth without there is good will *first*. If there were universal good will, there would be universal peace.   If anyone doubts it, let it be tried.

'The light you see might be going either way, might it not, it happens it is ascending.   It came about in this way.   This whole building with its gardens, was originally put up by the folk living hereabouts to serve as a pleasant place to receive the numerous teachers, and so on, who come from time to time from the higher realms to help us in a multitude of ways. Hence the chairs there, where the altar-stone would normally be.   The principal visitor will occupy the central chair, as you would guess, while the others would be taken by those come with him.

'Look round you, and what do you see; or rather, what don't you see?'

Roger turned about him: 'No memorials on the walls,' he enumerated, 'no religious pictures, no hymn-board, no candles or other ornaments.   In fact, it's just the empty shell of a church, but with comfortable chairs instead of hard pews.'

The side windows were also of coloured glass, and the rays of light passing in upon both sides produced the most delicate rainbow tints that met and mingled.

'Those two texts that you see, were put there at the express wish of the folk who were responsible for the whole building.   As with the rest of us here, they have a wholesome horror of war, most detestable scourge that ever could assail the people of earth. So they tried to think of some way in which to show their general concern, and at length they hit upon the scheme of taking that familiar quotation and emblazoning it upon the wails, right behind and above those high visitants when they are seated there, and in full view of every person as soon as he enters. They had it worked in mosaic, exquisitely, as you can see, in those bright colours, and made of it a permanent prayer by their thoughts. **That** is what you see ascending in that light, and it is never allowed to grow weak or feeble. You will always find it bright and strong. An infinitely small drop, my dear fellow, in an immense ocean of good thoughts; powerful enough in its way, though not powerful enough to stop or prevent war.

'You will have seen by now, Roger, that in these lands nothing is left undone merely for want of trying. Whatever the outcome of any enterprise, however hopeless it may seem from the start, yet an attempt will be made. We have our failures, and we have our successes too. War, my boy, is a large subject, and not a cheerful one, especially to you who are sampling the delights of the spirit world. Ruth and I don't want to depress you.'

'You won't do that, Monsignor; I like to know things, even if they're not too pleasant.'

At the 'west' end of the building there was a deep narthex upon which was reposing a large organ. It was not an instrument of advanced design or construction, and the pipes were arranged in their conventional order.

'A nice instrument, Roger. Anyone who wishes is at liberty to play upon it. Come along upstairs, and examine it, and perhaps Ruth will play us a tune.'

We mounted the stairs, and found ourselves in a wide gallery.

'There can't be electricity here, so would you like me to pump for you, Ruth?' Roger suggested.

'There's no need to do that, thank you, my dear,' said Ruth. 'You're right about our not having electricity. We've something much better.'

She pointed to a box-like receptacle on the floor a short distance from the organ.

'In there,' said she, 'is all we require. All I have to do is set that little machine in motion, and the air is sent along the trunk to the instrument.'

'Yes, but what makes the machine go?'

'Thought, Roger, thought; that's all,' answered Ruth with a smile. 'You know, you've hardly any notion yet what thought can really do.'

'No, I'm beginning to realize that !'

Ruth seated herself at the manuals and played a short piece that had been specially composed for her by one of our master-musician friends—a light, frolicsome lithe work, rather in the nature of a scherzo. When the final note had sounded, Ruth left the organ-seat, and taking Roger by the arm said, 'Now come and see what we've done.'

We left the building, and observing Ruth and myself gazing upwards above the roof, Roger did the same and was astonished to see, high up over the building, a huge sphere like a bubble, gently rotating upon its axis. Its colours, a delicate blue and pink, interweaved themselves without losing their identity.

'We should move a little farther away,' I said, 'then Roger will see the full effect. At present we're too much under it.'

We took up a position about a quarter of a mile distant where the full effect was superb. To Roger it was somewhat awe-inspiring to see this apparently fragile form suspended in the air with 'no visible means of support'.

'All music, Roger, makes a form of some kind when it is performed,' Ruth said, 'no matter what instrument it is played upon, though if I had played that piece on the piano, we should not have got such a large one as that. But we should have made a form; perhaps not as lovely. I've never played that piece on the piano, so I can't say what exactly would have happened. It was written for the organ, where one can get sufficient volume and variety of tonal effect. It's very beautiful, isn't it?'

'You know, Ruth,' said Roger, 'that's more frightening, even, than anything I've seen so far, though frightening isn't what I mean really.'

'No, old fellow, I know it isn't. I suppose awe-inspiring is the right term—it's a peculiar emotion whatever one calls it. Ruth and I both felt the same when we first experienced it, and even now we've not entirely grown out of it. I don't believe we ever shall. I hope not. If we did fail to respond there would be something wrong somewhere, and it wouldn't be the fault of the music. No, there's no question about it; we shall always feel some deep emotion whenever we hear and see music written by such masters as we have here, and they *are* masters, Roger.'

The lad was looking at Ruth with something like deep admiration, a kind of 'heroine-worship', one would say, that she should be able to achieve such a remarkable feat. For her part, Ruth was amused, and not a little touched by the lad's warmth of feeling, but she hastened to wave aside any credit to herself.

'What I've done is nothing, Roger. Anyone who can play can produce the same result. A mechanical instrument could do it, but no mechanical instrument could compose the music—that's where the credit must go, to the composer.'

'Did I understand you to say that a *master*-musician wrote the piece *specially* for you?'

'That is perfectly correct, Roger. Another surprise? It shouldn't be, you know, because, if you come to think of it, all those famous composers who have died, must be somewhere, mustn't they?'

'Yes, of course; that's rummy—l never thought of that.'

'Ah,' I remarked, 'I suppose that's because most folk regard musical composers as being only half human, if even that. That's why so many of them were half-starved when they lived on earth. When they left it, the people suddenly remembered them, and put up statues and monuments to them, and their works suddenly became very valuable. Things are a trifle better now on earth, and a composer need not actually starve, but if he has written some really good things they will be much more valuable after he's dead. At the present moment, earthly geniuses are notable by their absence. The real geniuses are all here. You've had an example, this minute, of the real genius. Even without being able to see that piece, it is a delight merely to listen to it.'

'How long will that ball remain there?' Roger asked.

'Normally,' Ruth told him, 'it would fade in a moment or so, but Monsignor and I put our thoughts together to charge it with a little more permanence so that you could see it in all its glory. When there are orchestral or other works following one another quickly, if the forms stayed too long they would all be mounted in a jumble on one another, and their shapes would be lost.'

# A Question of Age

'THERE's one thing that puzzles me,' declared Roger.

'Only one thing?' I queried. The lad is so good-natured that he never minds our mild bantering.'

We had returned to our house after our visit to the 'church' and Ruth's brief organ recital, and were sitting comfortably in the downstairs room where Roger caught his first glimpse of the spirit world.

'What is it that puzzles you, my dear fellow? State your case, as the lawyers say, and perhaps Ruth or I can throw some light on the matter.'

'It's this: how is it that everybody looks so young? I've not seen any old people anywhere?'

'Oh, yes, you have, Roger; but not in the way you mean, of course.'

'If I'm being too personal, Monsignor, tell me to mind my own business, but what would your age be?'

'You need have no fear about being too personal, my dear boy, in this matter of ages. We're not the least touchy over here. Even Ruth won't mind your asking such a question, and as you may know, the women folk on earth are sometimes a little sensitive on the subject! But here, no one cares, because one ceases to give the thing much thought. Still, it has its interesting side, especially to people like you and me, Roger—and Ruth, too—who like to "look into things" a bit.

'Well, now, as to my age. When I came over here I was forty-three, and I've been here for thirty-seven years—I know that because I have active interests in the old earth, and so have kept track of the passage of time. So, then, a simple sum, and you have the answer.'

'Good gracious,' the boy exclaimed. 'Then you are eighty!'

'Just so— a young man of eighty!'

'But you don't look anywhere near it.'

'I hope not. As a matter of fact, I scarcely look any different from what I appeared to be when I arrived here. A few alterations for the better, perhaps, but otherwise, no change.'

'And how old would you say I am, Roger?' asked Ruth.

'Careful, Roger,' I interposed, but he would not venture a guess.

'If you had said a hundred it wouldn't have upset me in the least. But I'm not that yet. Put it at about sixty-two, and you'll be right.'

'You don't look a minute older than about twenty-five,' returned Roger.

'Which was just my age when I came here.'

'Then what on earth age must I look?'

'Hardly beyond an infant in arms,' laughed Ruth. 'No, Roger, you look the same as you looked on earth, as far as age goes. In health, of course, vastly different, at any rate from those last few days. Poor dear, you were a very ill Roger then, but there's no comparison now. You mother would see in you now the lad she used to know.'

'You see how it is,' I said. 'In the spirit world age in years doesn't count. What happens is that the period known as the prime of life is the normal and permanent age. If one arrives here before that time, as you did and as many other do, even tiny infants, then you proceed gradually towards the prime of life, and there you remain. If you should come here after you've reached it—one may have gone far past it into the eighties and higher—then you revert, you return to the prime of life. In other words, you become younger.'

'That seems a sound idea.'

'It is a sound idea, but then all the ideas here are sound.'

We joined in laughter at our own condescending approval of the spirit world.

'Still, Roger,' I continued, 'for all our fun, the law that brings it about is a just one, and that's what you really meant. It's just in every way: for those who have passed the pre-scribed span on earth and for those who left it in early or very early infancy, or when they were your age, or Ruth's—and if it comes to that, mine as well almost.

'But I'll tell you one thing: you'll find it extremely difficult to guess a person's right age, which is to say, how long they have been in the spirit world, with the addition of the few years lived on earth.

'The longer you've lived in these lands, the shorter does the earthly period seem to become by comparison. Take Radiant Wing, for example. You couldn't possibly guess how long he has been here. If you had a little more knowledge— which, of course, will come to you as you go along—there would be certain indications that would help you in your guess.'

'No, I couldn't fathom how long he's been here. He looks in his prime—a young man. Yet when he speaks, and when you look at him closely, you can see that, without appearing old or elderly in any way, there is something that suggests weight of knowledge, or something like that.'

'Difficult to define, Roger, very. There's many an occasion, on seeing someone here, that you might say to yourself—if you should ever be so disrespectful—"he's no chicken". But there would be nothing to indicate positive agedness in such outward signs as wrinkles and lines, and all the other familiar landmarks of passing, or passed, years. How old would you say Radiant Wing is?'

'I can't hope to guess.'

'He's turned six hundred.'

'It's amazing, isn't it?'

'Not really. You remember Omar is two thousand if he's a day. His Egyptian aide is even older—in the region of five thousand years. What is it the psalmist says? *Longitudine dierum replebo eum*: I will fill him with length of days.

'This is an ageless world, Roger, and some of us, at any rate, would appear to be the same. No lined faces, no white or graying hair, no suggestions of that additional weight with which on earth we manage to burden ourselves, or on the other hand, no indications of shrivelling up and wasting away; no slowing down of our movements, or alterations in the pitch of our voices; no loss of mental vigour. No second childhood. Eliminate this melancholy catalogue, and you have us as we are, restored to a second prime, those of us that need it, instead of advancing into a second childhood.'

'How old would you say the spirit world is, Monsignor?'

'My dear fellow, that *is* a question! You know what is said: eternity can have no beginning. And eternity, as with immortality, is something that cannot be proved. The only thing you can do in this particular instance, is to try to find out what is the consensus of opinion on the matter, and there you will find that we are all of one mind, and that is that this world and ourselves with it, are eternal. We have the feeling of absolute permanence. If it were not permanent, then what is the use of all this? What is the use of continuing at all?

'No, my boy, everything here in these lands cries out against there being an end to this glorious life, and the still better life that lies in front of every one of us. And we, in these realms, have the assurance—did we need it—of those stupendous souls in the very highest realms. If they are not telling us the truth, which is an infamous and preposterous supposition, then there is no truth.

'But we have our own powers, Roger. There's that to be considered. We can ourselves create. You've not seen us really on the job, yet, doing that. Wait till you see one of the experts running up a house for someone to live in, and as with a house, so with a palace or anything still larger. We make all this for ourselves with that power that comes from the great Source. Doubtless, you might argue, suppose the great Source cut off the power, withheld it, what then? That idea is equally preposterous. The power has been sent down ever since the spirit world existed. And that brings us back where we started!

'There does come a time when figures cease to have much significance for the ordinary person. When you contemplate the astronomical proportions into which the nations' finances have developed, when money is reckoned in thousands of millions, these figures can convey nothing whatever to the average mind. It's doubtful if they convey much to the people who are responsible for them. At any rate, the earth folk are now accustomed to such rows of almost unending digits, that when universal ages are brought in, they should cause no surprise.

'The most one could say, Roger, in answer to your question as to the age of the spirit world, is that it existed *before* the earth world. That we know from high sources. Well, then, if the earth first came into being between three thousand and five thousand million years ago, as it has been computed, then that figure *may* convey something to your mind. I'm rather afraid it won't. It doesn't to me.'

'Nor to me,' said Ruth.

'Just so. All it can do is to suggest a gargantuan number of years. If the spirit world were in existence so long ago as that—*and we have every assurance that it was*—then there are existing people in these lands, *somewhere*, who can claim *at least* that gigantic number of years as *their* age. And that makes the rest of *us* seem like—what? A grain of sand in a whole vast desert of comparative spiritual stature.'

'This is staggering, Monsignor.'

'Yes, Roger, if you allow it to be, but the truth of the matter is, in practice, we don't. It's breath-taking when regarded in a row of figures, in thousands of millions, but what seems to me the most shattering and crushing of all, is the knowledge, upon universal proportions, of those person-ages I spoke about. You've not met or spoken with one yet, Roger. Ruth and I have, in common and in company with many others in these lands. We have even visited the high abode of the greatest of them all. The time will certainly come when you will have that privilege, too, Roger, here in these very realms, even in this very house. Omar is himself in personal attendance upon him; is, in fact, his right hand.

'You see what you've brought on your young head by asking a simple question!'

'I realize now it was a foolish thing to ask.'

'Oh, no my dear fellow; by no means. The difficulty is to find an answer, and it's right you should satisfy your mind, as far as possible, upon things as they occur to you.

'There is, as you will guess, an enormous amount of things that are not told us not because they are deep secrets, but because we have much to learn first. The fact is, that with our necessarily limited knowledge and posers of comprehension, we should fail to understand them in our present state of advancement.

'It is like your school books, Roger. You were obliged to start at the beginning. A peep at the end of them would reveal things far beyond your then capabilities, and so would convey no meaning whatever. We are in no different case here as regards innumerable problems or questions. So we jog along, and find we're none the worse off for not knowing the answers. Everything fits into its proper place in these lands, and none of us would be handicapped in our progression by lack of knowledge. The knowledge will be there at the right moment. In the meantime, there's no harm in our having as many discussions as we like among ourselves—as we're doing at this minute. If it's possible for us to have light thrown upon them—subject to the limitations I have mentioned—then the light will come, you can be sure of that.

'This is a sensible world, Roger, as you will have gathered; though if some earth folk were to be relied upon, or believed, in their wild fantastic notions, this would be one of the silliest places in the universe. How would you like to exchange this life for one that has all the appearances of a long continual Sunday?'

'I should hate it.'

'So would we all. But there *are* people on earth who regard that mode of existence as being the very height of spiritual felicity; Paradise, in fact.

'There is another point about this longevity of the spirit world and the prime of life. And that is, some of us would tend to change rather in outward appearance if by chance we should be old or elderly when we came to the spirit world. On the other hand, there has been very little change in both Ruth and me, on account of our respective ages at transition. You, Roger, will naturally move onwards towards the prime of life period, and some change will no doubt take place. Not much, but some.

'The prevailing earthly fashions or modes would have some little effect, at any rate in men, for there have been times on earth when bearded gentry were the rule. Now you may have noticed we don't indulge in such facial adornments here, though if you wished to grow a patriarchal beard down to your waist, or any other kind, there is nothing whatever to prevent you. There's no law "agin it". It might require some considerable courage. Certain of our friends might make very pointed remarks if I were to cultivate any facial decorations.'

'I should, for one,' said Ruth.

'Which I should at once ascribe to pure envy! You can see, Roger, how it is. Identity isn't lost, but it certainly can become obscured, as you might say. The man—or woman—when he is old looks very different from when he was young, and the man with a beard looks vastly changed without it. And those changes are not long in taking place. One soon shakes off the physical characteristics that belong to the earthly side of life, and puts on the spirit-world personality. Thereafter, longevity makes no difference.

'Take the comparative ages of Omar and his aide: there's a difference between them that can be reckoned as three thousand years of earthly time. Could you honestly say which of the two is the elder?'

'No, Monsignor; impossible.'

'It is the same with millions more of us.'

'What would .happen in the case of people whose features are very well known on earth?'

'Do you mean historical figures or contemporary?'

'I was thinking of both.'

'In the case of historical people, there are all sorts of factors. One is that there may happen to be no accurate picture of them on earth to which reference can be made. Artists have tried at different times, and built up some semblance from records containing a description of the particular person. Most of them are inaccurate—the pictures, I mean.

'So that you might find yourself talking to people here, and be totally unaware of the fact that on earth they were once very famous people. Their identity has, in such cases, become completely submerged, as far as externals go. Of course, the person himself is still that person, although greatly improved, as we all hope to be! The old painters did their best, and turned out faces that were at least human—which is more than can be said of so many of the present earthly painters! But the originals have changed beyond all recognition.

'What, after all, is earthly fame, of one sort and another? It depends upon what the fame rests. It is possible to see on the earth at present many whose fame rests upon a reputation of utter fatuity. That's not so much their fault as that of the empty-headed people who give them such generous support.

'There are people, too, whose earthly reputation and fame were of a very unsavoury kind, but who have since risen to the realms of light, and are profoundly glad that their portraits on earth are inaccurate delineations. Recognition, therefore, fails in these lands.'

# *A Lesson in Creation*

'How,' I asked Roger, 'would you regard this house and everything that's in it, and all that you can see from these windows? As something pretty solid?'

'I certainly should,' he answered. 'Why do you ask?'

'Because, my dear fellow, there are people on earth who will have it that all this is a *condition* built by thought, and therefore having no concrete existence, as they would term it. Odd, isn't it?'

'I think I can understand it, in a way,' said Roger, 'because when I woke up on your couch, it did occur to me that it might be a dream'

'Then what happened?'

'Well, I saw you sitting at the foot of the couch, and there was Ruth at my side, and you spoke sense.'

'Thank goodness for that!'

'You know what I mean.'

We laughed at the boy's confusion. 'Of course, Roger. You mean that the whole situation was sensible, and not the sort of crazy things that usually happen in dreams.'

'Yes, that's it. At once it was all very real. You remember I put my foot on the ground. After that there could be no suggestion that everything here is not real and solid.'

'Real and solid, Roger; that is the vital point. The trouble would seem to be that folk on earth have not yet fully realized the true significance of the power of thought. Within limits they have some idea, and a good idea, but it's my opinion that they don't carry the matter far enough.

'Take your mind back to the time when Ruth and I came into your bedroom on earth. We just came in, as it were. Nothing was solid to *us*. The walls meant nothing. And we meant nothing to you—as yet. Even when you did see us, we were pretty insubstantial. The whole of these lands were as yet invisible to you, though you did begin by seeing us.

'Then what happened? One life ended for you there, and another began—in your bedroom, or to be precise, in the spot where your room was situated, and we took charge of you for the time being. Had you remained awake—it was Ruth put you into a nice little nap—you would have seen what we two saw—a vapoury room, with rather vapoury people in it. We could have said with similar justification, that the room was only a condition, and not a state. But we know differently. That room was real and solid to your folks there in it. You had changed your condition, from earthly to spirit life, but you had not turned yourself into a state, nor had we done it for you. You see what I mean?

'Now, had you anything in mind about a future life? No, you've told us you hadn't, so that you could not have found yourself in some kind of thought creation of your own, based upon what you supposed the spirit world to be.'

'No, but couldn't I have found myself in some kind of state or condition that someone else had *created*?'

'Well said, my lad. That's precisely what did take place. So that, to use definite terms, it must be a solid type of place that others can see and feel and experience—and enjoy.'

'Then where comes the difference between this and the earth?'

'The difference lies in the fact that here there is no solid earth condition to interpose itself between us and our thoughts. Whatever is created or made on earth has to be thought about first, planned, perhaps drawings made if it is something a bit elaborate, and then fashioned by machinery or by hand, as the case may be. Here we dispense with the intermediaries, as it were, and let thought do the job, which it does very capably.

'Thought has direct action here. That's where the real difficulty is. Because thought has such direct action, folk on earth think that the results must be intangible, dream-like, and capable of being, or liable to be, dispersed upon the slightest provocation, or upon none at all. Our thoughts in these lands have far greater power and scope than on earth. To make things concrete on earth, one had to get past the thinking state. Here one is always in the thinking stage because that is the last stage, if you follow me.

'Immediately upon the thought there follows the concrete article. I don't mean for one moment that we merely think of what we need or desire, and hey presto, there it is. Dear me, no. This house, Roger, was carefully thought about, planned, and then the masons and builders got to work. But *their* work was performed by thought alone. There were no intermediaries in the form of the procuring of materials, and the erection of scaffolding, and so on. Those friends *thought*, and thought produced this very real and solid house.  And here it will remain.

'We're not sitting on nothing.  We're sitting in comfortable chairs, and they are resting on the floor.  This is not a thought condition we're living in—and a good thing, too!'

'Then if you want to make something, you have to learn how to make it; is that it, Monsignor?'

'Very much so.  Do you think you could make a table like that, this very minute?'

'I'm sure I couldn't.'

'No, neither could Ruth nor I.  Ruth makes tapestries—you've seen some of them here, Roger; but she makes them on a machine, itself made by an expert, with materials also made by experts.  But they're none the less real for that.  How do you suppose the flowers and things come?'

'I haven't the faintest notion.'

'Would you care to see some being made?'

'I should, very much indeed.'

'Then let us go and call on the man—or one of them—who does it.'

As we made our way thither we explained to Roger that the friend upon whom we were calling, keeps what on earth would be called a nursery-garden; that when he was incarnate he had done similar work.

'I imagined,' said Roger, 'that the flowers grew here in much the same way as on earth—from seed, and so on.  That doesn't appear to be so from what you say.  What happens, then?'

'Let us wait until we get there, Roger, and our friend will tell you all about it.  Look, now; you can see where the gardens are.

In front of us we could perceive great tracts of brilliant colours, each colour separate, stretching far away in field after field. There were trees of all kinds in every stage of growth, from mere saplings to veritable patriarchs. We followed a path that led directly to a large house.

As I had already sent a message to the 'owner' of the nursery, he was awaiting our arrival. Roger was therefore surprised when the opening words of our friend clearly indicated that he already knew of our impending visit. Ruth briefly told Roger about the thought process of sending messages, to which he replied by saying that that was something further that had to be investigated!

We introduced Roger to our host as a new arrival who was following the usual procedure of seeing things for himself.

'So you've come to see the flowers made, young friend. Well, you've come to the right place,' he said with a merry twinkle.

Roger had by now completely overcome any shyness he may have had, and plied people with questions with a right good will. He commenced operations at once upon our gardener friend.

'Do you supply the flowers for all these lands?' he queried.

'Oh, no. Only for this area, as you might call it. There's lots more people doing the work in other parts. This is just one. Now where shall we begin? First come and see some of our products.'

Surrounding us were hundreds of flower-beds each containing a different kind of flower, and each arranged in orderly rows.

'We don't make any attempt to be properly artistic in what we call our stock beds, though, mind you, the colours themselves attract great admiration, as well as the long lines of flowers and plants. It is the masses of flower and colour that folk find so fascinating. Our own gardens, over yonder, we laid out for pure pleasure purposes.'

We noticed particularly the enormous number of blooms that grew upon a single stem of each plant.

'You see,' explained the gardener, 'in the old earth plants the flowers fade in due course, and seed pods form, so that you might have half the stem with blooms and half with seeds. You can see for yourself that, without this happening, and the whole stem being filled with blooms for its right length, there's no comparison. There's nowhere else but here—I mean, the spirit world—where flowers could be grown like these.

'Cast your eye on those hollyhocks. Did you ever see such beauties as those—with blooms from the top reaching down all that way? And no fading or dying. That's how we make them and that's how they stay.'

As far as we could see were bed upon bed of such perfect flowers as incarnate eye never beheld. Ruth and I had visited this beautiful place often before, but to Roger it was new, and such a revelation as to hold him almost speechless.

There were flowers of every variety known on earth, all the old cherished blooms that have been familiar to earth folk time out of mind—the 'old-fashioned' flowers, as one liked to regard them: the hollyhocks and pansies, the snapdragons, Canterbury bells, and wallflowers, stocks, and a hundred other kinds. As may be imagined, the scent from this great collection was superb; not overpowering, but sufficient to make its presence pleasantly felt, and enjoyable.

'You can understand this work is more like a holiday when we compare it to the labour that would be required on earth for such large gardens as these. I doubt if there are any as big as these on earth, and these aren't the biggest by any means. Still, we have everything that may be called for here.

'As I was saying, it's more like a holiday here. We're not bothered with all the troubles of things on earth, the weather, for instance—most of all the weather; or the right soil; and everything to do with the planting, and so on. It's a long process on earth from the moment the seed is planted to the time you come to pick the blooms for the market. But here, bless you, we *make* our plant with its blooms already on it, in all varieties and mixtures of colours. We can have single blooms or double, as we fancy, or as others fancy. And once we've made them and planted them out, well, there's nothing more to do, so to speak. But we're not idle for all that—even if its merely showing people round.'

'You would think, Roger,' I said, 'that our gardener here had precious little to do. Don't be deceived. He is the genius behind all our gardens, the designer-in-chief. He and his colleagues, brothers in the art, are responsible for the loveliness of the many gardens you've seen.'

We followed our guide along path after path, from flowerbeds to avenues of trees and shrubs. The super-abundance seemed overwhelming, but our friend assured us that everything we saw would be put to good use, and was not there merely for display.

Roger put a question to him: 'If the flowers and trees never fade and die,' he asked, 'how is it so many are wanted? The demand must be enormous.'

'You're right; the demand *is* enormous. Some people like to expand their gardens, or put in new beds. That's one way we come in. Then there's the gardens in the city. They're often reconstructed or otherwise changed about. So we come in again. Then people feel the urge to change what's growing in their gardens, and we supply them with new stuff, bringing back here what they have discarded. When you come to look around you, you can see there's still plenty of room to make more beds—and fill them. Now come indoors, and see some of our treasures.'

We were shown into a spacious apartment containing many shelves filled with large volumes. Our friend took down one volume and opened it at random. It showed a picture of a tulip, exquisitely drawn in colour. It was not an artistic reproduction in the strict sense of the term; it was a purely botanical picture, without background, and revealed full details of the flower and its foliage, so that anyone viewing it would know exactly how the flower was composed. Especially true was the colouring of it, so we were informed.

'It is from these paintings that our pupils learn all the details of the flowers before they commence the actual process of creation. Before you can begin to build a flower, or anything else, if it comes to that, you must know precisely all the details necessary for a faithful reproduction. "Near enough" is not good enough. It's got to be perfect. And the only way to make it so is to know by heart every twist or turn of the object that is to be created. You could take it right off the drawing, so to speak; in fact, that is what the beginner always does. But afterwards, he will study the picture—or an original, if he prefers it—and that leaves him free, when the work commences, to devote his whole mind to the object in hand.

'In all these volumes you will find coloured pictures of every flower we make here, both the earthly kinds and those that belong to the spirit world alone.

'In addition to these books, we have the prints hanging separately on the walls in another room. That's done for the convenience of anyone who wishes to view them without looking through the volumes. Come across the hall into the big room.'

We entered a very large chamber where, hanging upon the walls, were magnificent pictures of every type of garden to be seen in these lands. It was impossible to assess the greater beauty of any one over that of another. They were all equally wonderful.

'Most of these gardens,' our host pointed out, 'have actually been built somewhere or other in this area. Inventive faculties don't seem to have any limit, as you can see.

'Some of these sketches have been presented to us from other nursery-gardens, in the same way as we pass on drawings and sketches that portray some particularly happy novelty. A regular exchange goes on, for you know, young friend, in these lands we are always on the move in things. We don't "stick in the mud"!' At length our gardener friend led us into a smaller room where there were a number of young people busily occupied, and we were told that these were pupils in the art of horticulture.

We perceived that Roger had all this time been immensely attracted and interested in what he was being show. Not that he had exhibited any signs of boredom hitherto, but here there was an especial attraction, which, to the eyes of Ruth and me—and the gardener—showed very plainly that he would like to take up this work himself.

Our friend at last brought us to the climax of our visit: the actual creation of a flower.

For this purpose he seated us around him, while he placed upon a table a small vessel similar to the ordinary flower-pot. Into this he poured some 'soil', and without further preliminary, he requested us to watch the vessel upon the table.

At first there was little to be seen beyond a slight haze of light round about the pot. Gradually, however this formed itself into a distinct shape, which one could see was the outline of a stem with a flower upon it. This became more and more firm, until there was the complete adumbrating of a flower, even to the colour, though this latter was as yet rather pale.

But there was sufficient formation to be able to observe unmistakably the kind of flower it was, namely a tulip.

The gardener rose from his seat, took up the pot, and examined it minutely, before he pronounced his satisfaction, and then passed it round for us to inspect.

It was a beautiful object, shapely yet delicate, so that one could see clearly through it. I handed it back to its creator, who placed it upon the table once more, and with one final effort of concentrated thought brought the flower up to its full solidity and colour, with apparently little effort.

'There you are, Roger. There's a nice flower for you. Can you see anything wrong with it?

The boy replied that he could see absolutely nothing whatever the matter with it.

'There is, though. Monsignor and Ruth know, but we've not let you into the secret yet.'

Roger re-examined the tulip, but again confessed himself unable to detect anything amiss.

'As a flower merely to look at, it's the best we can do, but there is something missing: there is no animation to preserve it. We can't give it—or any flower—*that*. That *must* come from another realm, and we don't ask for it until we are sure that what we have made is fitted to receive it.

'Oh, we make our mistakes, you know; especially my young pupil boys and girls. You expect to have some mishaps when you're learning, but no harm is done. We return the elements to their source, and begin again.

'Sometimes we find a petal, for instance, has not been shaped truly; perhaps one side of the bloom is a shade higher than the other, or the colour may not be exactly as we want it. And so we have to begin again.

'My students find an enormous amount of pleasure in their learning, but the greatest satisfaction comes when they are fully proficient, and can turn out a flower or plant as perfect as the picture.'

'How does the animation come?' asked Roger. 'Do you have to perform some sort of service for it?'

'Do you mean a religious service?'

'Yes, something of the kind.'

'Oh, no. What we do is to send to that higher realm I mentioned, where someone receives our message; after that, all we know is that there is a rapid descent of the power we ask for. Of course, originally, it comes from *the* Source, but it is passed on to us from another personage. It is a natural process and procedure, and the fact that we have created the flower or plant is sufficient. Our desire for its complete animation is fulfilled; our request is answered without fail, and without question. We shouldn't ask for it for an inferior article, though we could have it even for that, but our natural pride wouldn't allow us to do so.

'At first I examine all my pupils' work. If any slight modification or improvement is needed, that can be done, but if it's too bad for improvement, then it's started anew, and the misformed work is discarded.

'It's very simple when once you are in the running of it, so to speak. As with many other things, it's easy when you know how.'

'I shouldn't like to say *that*—at least as far as I'm concerned,' I said. 'I'm convinced I should turn out a flower such as had never been seen before, and was never likely to be seen again.'

'Oh, come now, Monsignor. Would you like to try for yourself?'

'Indeed, I should not. I should be far too nervous, especially with the three of you gazing at me—and waiting for trouble.'

They laughed at my frank expression of plain cowardice.

'As a matter of practice, we don't go about it that way. Every new pupil retires with me into our little sanctum, where we make our experiments and first essays at creation in seclusion. So there's no embarrassment at all.'

'Of course, my dear friend, I know that, but all the same I don't somehow think I should make a great success of it,' I affirmed.

'Would there be, do you think, a vacancy of any sort for another learner,' asked Roger, 'because, if so, I should very much like ——?'

'To become one,' said the gardener, finishing Roger's sentence for him. 'There's plenty of room, and to spare. But before we go into that, let me finish off this tulip. It won't take a moment. So.'

He held the tulip in his hand, and instantly we saw a flash of light descend upon it. It came and was ended almost before one realized it.

'Now,' said he, 'we have something very different. Smell.'

He gently waved the flower to and fro before us, and we were at once aware of the most subtle perfume.

'Place your hands round the bloom, friend Roger.'

Roger did so. 'Why,' he said, 'it's alive! I can feel the— what is it; sort of electricity?—running up my arms.'

'No, it's not electricity, but it *is* power. That is actually the life you feel, and it's passing some on to you, for your benefit. We've not finished yet. Put the pot on the table, then take hold of the stem of the plant, and give it a little shake, as though you were trying to shake a drop of water off the petals. That's the way.'

As Roger performed this simple action, a most perfect sound issued forth, as of the striking of a small silvery bell, of clear and sweet tone.

He repeated the experiment over and over again, such was his surprised delight.

'Do all the flowers make that sound when this is done to them?' he asked.

'All the flowers, and many other things beside. The water, for instance. You can bring out some lovely sounds from that when it is disturbed. But before the tulip was given life, it was silent.

'Well, now, you would like to join us. We shall be delighted to have you whenever you feel disposed to come. Ruth and Monsignor are showing you round for the present. There's plenty of time. See the world—our world—first, eh Monsignor?'

'That is so, Roger,' I said. 'Do you feel you want to start here immediately?'

'Oh, no, not this instant.'

'Good; then we can continue or perambulations, and see some more, and then our friend will be happy to make you one of his pupils. I can give you any details that you might want to know, without taking up too much of our friend's time.'

And so that matter was pleasantly settled, and another happy soul made happier still.

# The Man in the Cottage

'You mentioned other places, Monsignor,' remarked Roger, 'places that are not pleasant, as these are.'

'That is so, Roger,' I replied.

'Where are they?'

'As to their precise location, well, that is not so easy to define. As I expect you've noticed, the four points of the compass have no significance in these realms or anywhere else in the spirit world. That, as you will remember, was a matter that might have cropped up when you once asked if it were possible to lose one's self here. Still, we could soon take you to those unpleasant places. Do you really wish to see them?'

The boy was silent for a moment. 'Perhaps I had better be guided by Ruth and yourself; I mean, guided by your advice.'

'Then, my dear boy, if you wish for our suggestions, I'm sure Ruth will agree with me that it were much better that you keep away from the dark regions for some time yet.'

'Monsignor is perfectly right, Roger. Don't go there. You know we will do anything for you that we possibly can, but those beastly regions are not for you yet. Later on, perhaps. Accept our word for it—there are thousands who could corroborate us—that you wouldn't feel at all happy about it afterwards. You know how, on earth, deep curiosity would lead us towards looking at something or other we were pretty sure we should afterwards regret having seen. We would give in, and our first impressions become verified. Here's just such another instance.'

'There's this can be said, Roger. Those dark realms are not the theological hell to which people are condemned for all eternity—once in, never out again. Every person, who at present is an inhabitant of those terrible places, has the free choice to emerge from them whenever he changes his mind. He can work his way out in precisely the same way as *we* can work *our* way from these lovely lands into still lovelier. The law is the same there as here, and applies to us all—there and here. And here is a living witness to what I say.

'Do you see that trim cottage over there, Roger, with the two tall trees near it? Well, I'm revealing no secrets when I tell you that the dweller in that cottage once lived in an awful hovel, not actually in the dark realms, but in the dismal, bleak regions that lie close to them—the sort of twilight of the dark lands themselves. Ah, our friend has seen us.'

We had perceived the owner of the cottage sitting in his garden, and now he was waving to us.

'Shall we take Roger to see him, Monsignor?' Ruth suggested.

'That would be a capital notion, my dear, if Roger doesn't mind listening to our friend's story. It's not a long one, nor is it frightening or anything of that sort. But I must tell you this, that it was largely due to Ruth that he was able to turn the corner, as it were, and emerge from his unhappiness. So you can readily imagine that he regards Ruth as something only very slightly less than an archangel.'

Ruth laughed.

'Well,' said Roger, 'I think that the gentleman is entirely right. He's a very good judge, anyway. I can easily understand how he feels, for both of you have done so much for me already, even in this short period.'

'No, my boy. We've done nothing that millions of others would not have done. But we must spare Ruth's blushes.

'I'll tell you what, Roger. If you feel like listening to our friend's story you will be doing him a very good turn, because he feels that he owes so much for the help he's been given that he can't do enough in return, and telling others about his rehabilitation, he believes, is some small way of showing his gratitude. Bless him, his heart's in the right place, and you'll find he doesn't spare himself, either.'

'I thought for a moment you were going to say "doesn't spare the horses".'

'Roger! How *could* you!' exclaimed Ruth. 'If Monsignor ever puts that down on paper—and he's liable to—what would some of the earth folk say?'

'"Trivial rubbish", my dear; all of it,' I said. 'I hope you won't think, Roger, from what I've said about our friend here that he's a trying old bore. Far from it. But in this case I think you'll find his simple story will answer a number of questions for you without your having to ask them.'

'And if I didn't know otherwise I should say that will save you a great deal of bother, one way and another,' said Roger with a grin.

'Glorious, Roger; that's a good one against Monsignor,' said Ruth.

'He included *you* in that statement, Ruth,' I pointed out.

By this time we were within hailing distance of our friend, and he came rapidly towards us.

'Ruth—Monsignor,' he cried with evident delight; 'this *is* a pleasure. It seems a long time since I saw you both. And who is our young friend? I've not had the pleasure of seeing him before.'

We introduced Roger, and explained that one of the reasons why we had not seen him of late was that we were showing Roger round his new land.

'How are you?' asked Ruth.

'Why, my dear, I never felt better in my life. Is it possible, do you think, for us ever to feel better than we do now?'

'That's something I should very much like to know as well, sir,' said Roger.

'There you are, my dear. Here's this young gentleman who firmly supports me in my demand. Now then, what does that wise head say?'

Our friend slipped his arm through Roger's.

'Why, I don't know,' Ruth answered with a smile, 'but I don't see how we could feel any better than we do already. Perhaps it's all a matter of comparison.'

'That must be it, and compared with what I *once* felt, this is perfection. It might be called "Paradise regained", if I were at all sure that I ever had it to lose and regain. But come inside, and let our new friend see what a spirit world country cottage looks like.'

This small dwelling was as neat and trim inside as it was outside, and everything was arranged with the greatest taste and refinement, and with yet an eye upon solid comfort and enjoyment. In the apartment which we entered directly from the garden, the furniture was of the ancient style, well constructed and pleasant to behold. It was kept in a high state of polish, and reflected the large bowls of flowers that were everywhere displayed. The other rooms, both upstairs and down, were similarly appointed, and altogether the whole dwelling revealed the natural pride and devoted care of its owner.

'I have no shame in telling you, Roger, my friend, that this is a very different place from the one I inhabited when I first came in to the spirit world, as Ruth and Monsignor will tell you, and, of course, Edwin. Where is Edwin, now? Why isn't he with you?'

'He has been very busy of late,' Ruth replied, 'and none of us has seen much of him beyond a fleeting visit. Roger was one of our own cases—do you like being referred to as a case, Roger?—and we thought we would take time off and show him things.'

'Doing for him, what Edwin did for you and Monsignor. Do you remember your first visit to *me*?—but of course you do. *I* shall never forget it.'

'If you feel so disposed, tell Roger about it.'

Our friend reflected for a moment. Why, yes,  if you wish,' he said, 'but he should know first how I came to live in such a place, such an awful place, as that was.

'When I lived on earth, Roger, I was a successful business man. Business was my preoccupation in life, for I thought of precious little else, and I considered all means right in my dealings with others, provided such means were strictly legal. As long as they were that, I deemed the rest did not matter. I was ruthless, therefore, in gaining my ends, and coupled with a high degree of efficiency, I achieved great commercial success.

'In my home, there was only one person to be thought of, and that was myself. The rest of the family did as they were told—and I did the telling.

'I always gave generously to charity when I thought I should derive the greatest benefit and credit for myself, for I did not believe in anonymity as far as I was concerned. If any donations were to be given I saw to it that my name was sufficiently prominent. Of course, I supported the church in the district where I lived, and at my own expense had some portions added to the building, with proper emphasis upon the donor.

'The house I occupied was my own, and of such size and situation as befitted my position in the world. In every respect, Roger, I regarded myself as a god. It wasn't until I came to the spirit world that I discovered that I was one—made of *tin*, the sorriest, shabbiest god that ever existed.

'I was only a year or two past middle-life when disease overtook me, and at length I "died".

'I had every reason to know that I was given a magnificent funeral, with all the customary trappings, suitable mourning, and so on, though I have since learned that there was not one soul who cared a brass farthing that I had gone. On the contrary, they were glad. Some declared that the devil had got his own at last. Others said that I was the one justification for the existence of hell, and that the earth was the sweeter for my removal. Such was the fragrant memory I left behind me. And where was I, do you think, Roger, during all these sad lamentations at my departure?

'I awoke to find myself in the dirtiest, wretchedest hovel you can imagine. I could take and show you the place this moment, for it's still standing. The house—the hovel—was small, and seemed all the more so after the large establishment I was accustomed to on earth. It stood in a horrible, bleak spot, without garden or any living thing round about. The inside was in keeping with the outside, poorly, meanly furnished.

'Seeing it for the first time, some might have thought that poverty was the trouble. So it was—*poverty of the soul*—for I had never done anything for anyone on earth, except it be for my own ultimate benefit, not theirs.

'The very clothes I was wearing were threadbare and soiled. In this dingy hole I found myself, smouldering with rage that I should, in some inconceivable fashion, have been reduced to such a state of squalor. I didn't seem able to leave the premises; I felt glued to the house. I gazed out of the windows, and could see nothing but barren ground, with a belt of mist not far away. A grim, dismal outlook, in a literal sense. I stormed and raved, and it was in this situation that Edwin found me.

'He came to me one day, and I treated him as I had been accustomed to treat those whom I considered my inferiors on earth. Now Edwin was the last person to be spoken to in that fashion. You've not met him, have you, Roger, my boy? A quiet, kind personality, but firm. He stood no nonsense from me, I can tell you, but in my then frame of mind he could make no headway.

'I was consumed with anger, an anger that was aggravated by the fact that I did not know whom to blame for my present situation. The last person I thought of blaming was myself. However, I found some measure of consolation in assigning the responsibility where I fancied the largest share of it should rest, and that was upon the Church, for I felt I had been misled. Had I not given generously to the Church, and had I not been led to believe that my donations, and they were upon a considerable scale, would stand me in very good stead when my time came to depart from earth? I considered I had been done a grave injustice, and that the Church, of which I regarded myself a most ornate pillar, had flagrantly misled me, and that I was called upon to pay for its mistake.

'To whom was I to turn in my difficulties? I was perfectly well aware of what had taken place; in other words, that I was "dead". But the mere knowledge of that was of precious little use.

'I suppose I must have emitted some kind of thought in request of assistance. Whatever it may be, I perceived a man coming towards the house, and that man was Edwin. It was the first of many visits he paid me, and every one with the same result. I was adamant. I was also extremely rude. But Edwin was not the sort to be intimidated by one such as me, and he gave me as good—better, in fact—as I gave him! He could always have the last word, so to speak. He simply marched out of the house and left me when I became too intractable.

'At length he returned, but this time not alone, for he brought with him two friends (and another whom I had sometimes seen in the area), the same two friends who are looking after you, Roger—Monsignor and Ruth.

'Glancing back now, I know that visit was the turning point. Ruth and Monsignor stood in my room, very discreetly in the background, while Edwin spoke to me. I began to feel a trifle less angry, and my eyes were continually drawn towards Ruth, when I had first glimmerings of light, if I may so express it.

'Ruth's presence served to remind me that I had a daughter of my own, though I had treated her equally abominably with the rest. There was no physical resemblance between

Ruth and my daughter, it was more one of temperament, as far as I could judge. Whatever it was, I already began to feel differently. That, combined with all that Edwin had spoken to me on so many occasions, had its effect. After my visitors had gone, a terrible loneliness came over me, as well as deep, dark remorse, so intense that I cried aloud in my despair for Edwin's presence now, which I had so often spurned with contempt, for I had put in some good thinking.

'You can imagine my joy and surprise when I perceived Edwin coming towards the house almost upon the instant of my cry. I met him at the door, and as he would tell you himself, I was a changed man.

'The first thing I did was to thank him for coming so expeditiously—and I was not much accustomed to thanking people for anything. The next, was to apologize to him for all I had said and done to him. But he waved my words aside with a brilliant smile upon his face that clearly bespoke his great pleasure that, at last, I was on the way to being something very different from the inflated egoist and spiritual blackguard that I was when I arrived in the spirit lands.

'Edwin at once sat down with me and proceeded to discuss ways and means of getting me out of the hell-hole that was my abode. A course of action was decided upon. Edwin did the deciding, for I put myself entirely in his hands, and for the present it was arranged that I should remain where I was for a brief while, and that I had but to call him and he would come.

'After he had gone, I gazed round upon my house, and in some extraordinary manner it seemed much brighter than it was. It was unquestionably less dingy, and my clothes were less shabby, and that discovery helped to make me feel a great deal happier.

'I will not bore you with all the struggles, hard struggles, I had to make up for all that was past. It was hard work, but I never lacked friends. I don't need to look farther than this room to see two, at least.

'Well, Roger, you see me now, as unlike my old self as day is to night, still working hard, and glad of it. My work? Why, doing for others what Edwin did for me—and for the same kind of people! It's easier to handle them when you've been one of them yourself,' our host added with a chuckle.

'There's one consolation,' he went on; 'they've pretty well forgotten about me on earth. Otherwise they'd think of me as being far worse than old Scrooge, and would point out that, at the last, Scrooge reformed and became a decent citizen, while I went to my end unrepentant. Perfectly true, but they don't know that I've changed my views somewhat since then, and they'd not know me for the man I was.

'Still, maybe they'll find out one day, and, my word, there'll be surprises all round!'

# Philosophers' Folly

'Would you, Roger, describe these realms of the spirit world as a dreary imitation of the earth?" I asked our young friend.

'Good gracious, no. Whoever said they were?'

'The particular gentleman I have in mind, though not the only one of his kind, lives on earth, and is regarded by his friends, and one or two people who make money out of him, as a philosopher. The truth is that he knows a little about something and never hesitates to say a great deal about everything. His friends and admirers naturally consider him a perfect oracle, and pause upon his every word—I believe that is the expression. He is always ready with pontifical declarations upon every subject on earth. Sooner or later a subject not on earth is bound to crop up. Somebody will ask him if he believes in a "hereafter", and if so, what manner of place does he think it to be. That is the moment when the trouble begins.

'The great philosopher—and there are many whose title is accorded them upon the flimsiest grounds—knows nothing about the matter whatever, but that is no hindrance, and so he refers to literature dealing with the subject which he has never read, but has only heard about very sketchily. One of his most fatuous utterances is embodied in the question I put to you a moment ago: that the spirit world is a dreary imitation of the earth, which in his estimation, is a vastly superior place in which to live.

'Another objection which he raises concerns the quality and substance of the spiritual teachings that are sent to the earth from time to time.

'Do you remember that scriptural text, Roger, about loving one another? Good sound stuff that, eh?'

'Oh, yes. I heard sermons on the text, sometimes, when I went to church.' 'Which, I believe, was not very often. I'm referring to the church-going, not to the sermons on the text.'

Roger and Ruth both laughed. Our wit and humour may not be of a high, scintillating order, but then, it is not meant to be. Among ourselves we utter the same kind of pleasantries such as would be, and are, customary among friends in their own domestic circles on earth. And, I would have you know, we like to have our domestic circles here in these lands of the spirit world. We prefer to retain our mild jokes, however small they may be judged to be. Humour is the essence of this life. We take pleasure in making our friends and companions smile, as we ourselves are pleasured at *their* sallies. In other words, we are human, despite earthly ideas to the contrary. Doubtless much of what I am here setting down for you will be regarded as trivial rubbish. At least there is this to be said for it: it is not nearly as trivial or such rubbish as most of the grandiose utterances of earthly philosophers when they give their opinions of the spirit world and of us who live in it. What those same gentry think about affairs when they themselves come to live here, is another thing altogether.

'Now, Roger; when you heard those sermons on brotherly love, you thought it was good sound teaching, and beyond dispute, didn't you?'

'Yes, certainly.'

'And you were right. The original precept came from a man who *knew* what he was talking about. And our great philosopher would have been in complete agreement with the preacher in this case, that brotherly love is essential, and so on. It is essential, and spirit teachers have "harped upon that theme" time out of mind, and they will continue to do so, as long as there is an earth world to speak to. But what do you suppose is the comment upon such spirit world teachings when considered by at least one of these renowned philosophic gentlemen?'

'I've no notion.'

'It's this: "*frowzy religious uplift*". Elegant, isn't it? Can't you observe the stupendous mind at work? The parson preaches brotherly love to him from his pulpit, and he is suitably impressed and in full agreement. The spirit teacher tells him about it, and it becomes frowzy uplift.'

'Monsignor feels rather keenly on the subject, Roger,' observed Ruth, 'as we all do here, because sooner or later one of these gentlemen is bound to come our way, and that means hard work, and very tedious work for whoever is deputed to look after him.'

'You see, Roger, the trouble is not alone with these gentry themselves. Their pernicious views are read and absorbed by their rather tattered following, and treated as profound truths, so that if nothing intervenes in the meantime to make them alter their opinions, there will be others arriving here in a similar state of ignorance.'

'In other words,' said Roger, 'the mistakes of the earth have to be put right here.' 'That's exactly it. In your own case, it was an absolute holiday for Ruth and me. What so complicates individual instances is where the new arrival knows nothing about this life, but has wrong ideas about it. You knew nothing, and fortunately had no ideas at all. I don't say that derogation—you know that, my dear fellow. What you did have was a dear mind, free of all silly notions—even to the extent of harps and wings.

'One of the most senseless charges brought by these learned gentry is that all the communicators from the spirit world are English, so that, in effect, the spirit world is wholly English, to the total exclusion of all other nations.'

'People of other countries might say the same.'

'Exactly. The Frenchman, for instance, might say that the whole spirit world seems to be French because in France all the spirit communicators are French. The very same thing could be said throughout the whole earth world. Can you imagine what would happen if a company of these highly intelligent and sceptical philosophers were to meet, one from every nation? They would each be in somewhat of a difficulty, for each would wish to establish his country's claims upon patriotic grounds, so to speak, but at the same time would lodge the complaint that the spirit world seemed to belong to his country alone. The proceedings would possibly have that familiar appearance to be observed in international conferences for the preservation of peace.'

'I suppose people of other nations die in the same way that we've done.'

'You suppose very rightly, my boy. A statement of the obvious, but not so obvious that our philosophic sages are able to perceive it.'

'Is this part of the spirit world English, then?'

'What would you think purely from appearances?'

'I should say, subject to the differences between this world and the earth, that there is a most decided leaning towards the old home landscape.'

'There is; and the houses bear a resemblance as well. We've not travelled very far afield as yet. So far you've not seen hills of any great height, nor have you seen mountains. But they are here. As to the people, whom have you met so far?'

'Well, there's Ruth and yourself, and you have spoken of Edwin.'

'All three of us English like yourself.'

'Then there is Radiant Wing, and Omar and his friend.'

'Exactly. The first an American Indian; the second, Chaldean; and the third, Egyptian. That's almost international in itself. You left out our cottage friend. He's another Englishman.

'The question is: among what nation did you—or would you—expect to find yourself after leaving the earth?'

'Why, it has never occurred to me. Among English people, I suppose.'

'Do you speak any other languages than your own?'

'Not one. A smattering of school Latin, perhaps.'

'It would have been decidedly awkward for you if you had awakened to find yourself among the Chinese, for instance.'

'Probably scared the life out of me.'

'Dear me, why? The Chinese are delightful people, kind and thoughtful, and always ready to help. You see, my dear fellow, that what you say points the stupidity of these philosopher gentlemen in their false notions that the spirit world must be an exclusively English one. There isn't one of them who would not feel much the same about it as you have this minute described.

'Ruth and I have met some of them, and they were profoundly glad to hear their own tongue, the English tongue, spoken in the same way as we spoke to you. And the same thing applies to the Frenchman, and the Chinaman, and all the rest.

'As you know, personal communication by the thought process obviates any difficulty in the language question. That process is without nationality. But when folks are awakening in these lands they use their vocal organs, and so do we. That's natural.

'What were your own impressions when you opened your eyes in our room beside the open window?'

'Well, I certainly had an at-home sort of feeling. The room was the kind I was familiar with, and the view through the window was most certainly familiar too.'

'Precisely. That's as it should be. So you see, there's law and reason behind all this, and nothing that the "wise" folk of the earth can say or think will alter it.'

'Then the other nations must be living somewhere else-that's a foolish thing to say. Of course they must.'

'They are, Roger. Every nation on earth has some position and location in the spirit world. People like to be among their own kind, and there's no reason why they should not be. Would it be right, do you think, or good policy, to force people of one particular nation or national temperament upon that of another? Not at first, at any rate.

'Then, as to the country itself. Nations prefer their own type of country however delightful that of others' may be. Here, they can find it. And that's right and natural too.'

'What about Omar and his friend?'

'Ah, they come into another category. Where they live nations have no significance, for the people themselves are above or beyond nationality. Radiant Wing is just such another. In the realm proper to him, he loses his precise nationality though not his racial individuality, if you understand what I mean.'

'I'm afraid I don't.'

'That's not your fault. It's mine! What I mean is that Radiant Wing will retain his particular cast of features, in the same way as Omar will, but that the nation of which he was a former member will have no significance for him, to the extent that Radiant Wing and Omar regard themselves as of no nation and of all nations, as it were.

'There's no end to the objections which these philosophic geniuses raise upon one matter or another.'

'I noticed that Omar and his friend both spoke English, and without a trace of accent too.'

'That is one of the objections I referred to. Can you think of any reason at all why Omar shouldn't speak English, or any other language?'

'None whatever if he wishes to.'

'*If he wishes to.* There you have it, Roger. If his particular work would be made easier, or indeed, made possible, by his doing so, then do it he will.

'As it happens, Omar has friends on earth, mutual friends, as a matter of fact. It became necessary for him to speak with those friends. At first he spoke no English, and they certainly knew no word of Chaldean. What was to be done? It was obvious from the outset that they couldn't learn Chaldean, but it was equally obvious that he could, with the greatest facility learn the English language. He did so without the slightest inconvenience to himself.

'You know what the memory can do here, Roger. Once something goes into the mind, there it stays. Why, Omar could learn any language well, so as to speak it fluently, while the earth folk are thinking about it. You will recall that

Radiant Wing knows sufficient of our native tongue to make himself comfortably understood for the purpose of his work on earth. Omar also wanted to make himself understood, but in a different way, and more extensively. He wished to cover a wide range of matters as lucidly as possible, and so he went deeply into the task of learning English. The very same applies to us all here. If you, my boy, wish to learn any language, whether to use it actively—I mean, conversation-ally—as well as to read literature in that language there is no power that can stop you. You are at liberty to begin this moment. Thousands of us don't, though, because there is no reason for us to do so.

'You know, Roger, the higher you go up the spiritual ladder, the less you think about nationality—and language, as such, unless there is work to be done on earth that involves the use of another tongue than your own.'

'How does one get to another country here?'

'In several ways. Shanks's mare is one of them.'

'*Monsignor*; what's this? How can you reprove Roger for using slang, when you use almost as bad yourself?' exclaimed Ruth laughing.

'You see, Roger, what a thoroughly bad influence you are. Here have I been carefully picking my way through the language so as not to use a single word or term that would be frowned upon by those folk on earth who think we should speak as though we were addressing an œcumenical council or something equally boring. Ah, well. "Evil communications corrupt good manners", I suppose.

'There is no difficulty in getting to other countries in these realms, or to be more exact, to those parts where folk from earth lands have their dwellings.

'You were thinking of frontiers mostly, weren't you? There *are* no frontiers. You may come and go as you please, and what's more, you'll be as welcome there as the inhabitants of those parts are welcome here. In fact, if you wander along you would hardly perceive you were "there", except for some slight difference in the landscape perhaps, and in the dwellinghouses.

'There is only one kind of barrier you'll come across in this world, and that is the barrier between one realm and another, and that's invisible, or practically so. An increase or diminution of the light, as the case may be. If there were not that, certain unpleasant, extremely unpleasant, elements would be tempted to overrun the regions next above them. And perhaps some of us would be tempted to develop ideas above our station, as the phrase used to be. It is a natural law that works in this way, and like all such laws it works without any breakdown, fuss, or trouble. That's the beauty of it. No question of difference of opinion, or insistence upon rights. There's no arguing with a natural law. I've yet to hear of anyone arguing with the law of gravity on earth. It would be a one-sided argument in any case, and probably end in disaster.

'As far as at least these particular realms are concerned, you might call them Cosmopolis with every justification, for you'll meet people of every nationality under the sun here, some of them coming and going, and some staying.'

'I can understand the coming and going, but how staying?' Roger asked.

'The best way to answer that is to give you a practical demonstration, though you've had one already, without knowing it.'

'Have I?'

'Yes; our old friend Radiant Wing.'

'Doesn't he belong here, then ?'

'Not by any means.'

'This is rather puzzling.'

'Shocking.'

'Monsignor is a terrible torment to you, Roger. Don't take any notice of him. I know what he means. Come along and we'll take you on another visit.'

'That's right. A visit that would be worth a fortune if it could be made on earth.'

With which cryptic utterance we took our young companion upon a social call at some distance from our home.

# A House in the Forest

'Now, Monsignor, will you please explain to me, in simple words if you wish, what you meant by "some staying", when you spoke of people of other nationalities?'

'That's right, Roger,' said Ruth; 'be firm.'

'Of course, my dear fellow. There's no mystery. What I meant was that it is sometimes the case that people dwell in certain realms here, when, by virtue of spiritual progression, they are entitled to live in a higher one.'

'Then why do they stay here?'

'Because, Roger, there may be very sound reasons for their staying. Some may elect to abide here for purely private reasons, reasons of affection between two individuals. It may transpire that two people, between whom there is a strong bond, might belong to different planes of progression, and therefore inhabit different realms. In such cases it is not

uncommon for the one entitled to live in the higher realm to
remain with the one who has not yet advanced, until such time
as the latter has progressed, and then, together, the two
mount to their new realm, and so continue unseparated.
That's one instance.

'There's another, and I believe more common one, and
that is where a certain occupation keeps people so absorbed
they prefer to work in the less high realm.  Our friend Radiant
Wing is such a case.  They are working for humanity still
incarnate, Roger, and although they spend a great deal of time
here in these regions, yet they constantly travel to their own
homes in the higher realms, and so they are residents of both
realms.  They're leading double lives!'

'Doesn't that sound too awful for words,' exclaimed
Ruth.

'Doesn't it!  And thousands of folk on earth are leading
double lives too, if it comes to that.  Their waking time spent
on earth, and their sleeping time spent in the spirit world.
There's a grand meeting of friends and relatives that way,
Roger.  But that's another story.'

We had already covered some distance when we reached
a part of the country that was well-wooded, and we entered a
very pleasant pine forest.  At length we came upon a clearing,
and before us was a most attractive house, of no great height,
but broad, as though several bungalows had been placed
together to form the one structure.  There were several large
masses of banked flowers to be seen, but no attempt had been
made to lay out the grounds surrounding the house into
anything like formal gardens.  There was an element of
wildness about the place, without, however, any suggestion
of disorderliness.  To the beholder it seemed to betoken a
haven of rest and quiet, though this was not in any sense
exceptional, since it is possible to attain absolute rest and

quiet even in the heart of the city without the slightest difficulty.

Ruth and I had visited this house upon many occasions, but it was new to Roger, and so, in respect thereof, our host was waiting for us at his house-door.

'Well, my dear Monsignor, and Ruth, too,' said he; 'you've come at the right moment, for I've something for you—at least, for Ruth.'

We introduced Roger, and briefly explained our proceedings and mission. There was an exchange of warm greeting between our friend and Roger, and we were at once invited within doors. 'Call our friend *Peter Ilyitch*,' I whispered to Roger, 'and look for surprises.'

One of them was not long in presenting itself. We were shown into a spacious apartment that was both sitting-room and work-room. Close to a wide window there was a large table upon which were disposed many sheets of music-manuscript, some of which had already been written upon, while a further quantity of unused paper was ready waiting, and it was evident that actual work was in progress. Along one wall was a commodious couch upon which an old friend of ours was seated, and who rose upon our entrance. He was presented to Roger as Franz Joseph and then resumed his seat.

What instantly attracted the attention of our young lad was Franz's companions. For upon the couch there was our undoubted old acquaintance, the puma, with whom Franz Joseph was now playing, while upon the arm of the couch was to be seen the little grey sparrow, who was industriously employed exercising his lungs in a vast deal of twittering. 'You've met before, it's plain to see,' said Peter Ilyitch, for the bird had at once flown to perch upon Roger's outstretched finger.

We asked Peter what the pair were doing here in his house.

'Why,' said he, 'I was at their home one day, and witnessed their amusing capers. While I was doing so, some music ran through my head that exactly fitted their antics. I thought it was rather too good to miss, and so I borrowed the pair of them from Radiant Wing, so that I could have them on the premises here, and watch them at my leisure. He has very kindly given me a sort of indefinite lease upon them. Their performances are never exactly the same. I expect you know, Roger, that Radiant Wing is Curator-in-Chief and Friend-at-Large to them, acting by special commission for his two friends on earth, who between them are the particular friends of these two "imps of mischief". I was at work on that music when you arrived.'

'Does that mean that we've seriously interrupted you?' asked Ruth.

'By no means, dear lady,' answered Peter. 'When I said I had something for you, I was referring to this very piece of music. The piano version is already completed. I thought perhaps you would like to have it. What I'm working on now is the orchestral arrangement, which I believe will be decidedly effective. It will differ only slightly from the piano version. Fuller, and with a few more frills and so on. Is Roger interested in this sort of thing?'

'Yes very. I played the scherzo you wrote for me, on the organ—the sphere, you know, and he was full of delight, and questions. That's one of the reasons for our present call, apart from wishing him to meet you. He doesn't suspect—at least I don't think he does—who you are, though Monsignor did caution him to look for surprises. He's had one already with the two pets. I'm sure he doesn't know who Franz is either.'

'Well, you know, my dear, we have changed a little since we came here.'

Roger was amusing himself with Franz, the puma, and the bird, and was oblivious to our conversation.

Presently Ruth called to him. 'Roger, dear,' said she, 'you remember the piece I played for you at the church? Peter has written another for me.'

Roger joined us at the table, and was now gazing very earnestly from Peter Ilyitch to a bust standing upon a side table. It was of a man in middle age, and wearing a neatly trimmed beard. Peter was amused at Roger's obvious attempt to match the two.

'You feel you can trace some relationship, Roger?' queried Peter. 'You're perfectly correct. That was how I looked when I was on earth. It's not vanity that leads me to keep that bust here, but solely the beauty of the workmanship.'

It was an exquisitely wrought piece of sculpture.

'It was done by someone who knew me as I was, and preferred to model it on those lines,' Peter continued. 'Do you think I've improved, Roger?'

'My goodness, sir,' answered Roger, 'that's an awkward question. If I say yes, it would imply there was room for improvement. If I say no, you haven't improved—oh, heavens!'

The boy was lost in confusion, and there was a burst of laughter from the rest of us, not the least from Peter himself. He was, of course, now in his prime of life, in precisely the same way as Franz had reverted to a similar period of external youthfulness.

Roger was very apologetic for his seeming curiosity, but he could not resist asking Peter what was contained in the many large volumes that were to be seen upon the shelves. To those unacquainted with the manuscript of orchestral scores, the volumes might have an unusual appearance in their size. It was explained that they constituted the works of our present host.

Roger was astounded at their enormous quantity. 'There is nothing remarkable about that, my dear friend,' said Peter. 'You see, it's some considerable time since I first came here to live, and I've not exactly been idle in the meantime. It amuses us greatly when we hear the announcement made on earth before a broadcast performance, that "this is the last work composed by so-and-so". *The last work.* Naturally, one knows what is meant, but it sounds so funny to us, especially when one glances at those shelves. Is it positively believed, I wonder, that once we've left the earth, we've stopped composing?'

I hastened to assure him it was so.

'That is why they put up statues and monuments to us, my dear friend,' said Franz Joseph. 'They think we are finished and done for; not a note left in us. And now they are perfectly certain they know what was in our minds when we wrote any piece, large or small. If any of us had given the plain reason: to keep off starvation, they wouldn't have approved of that. Not nearly mystic enough. Ah, well. *This* is the life. What do you say, my friends?'

There was no need to affirm our complete agreement!

'Now, Peter,' Franz added, 'play your new piece. I should like to hear it again myself.'

Peter went across to a grand piano standing in a corner— a handsome instrument—and commenced to play. I will not essay the impossible by attempting to describe what our friend played. To give a description of any piece of music in mere words is a useless and fruitless task, as it conveys to the reader precisely nothing. The most that can be done is to give a series of musical technicalities and details which in the end indicate precious little. Suffice it that the music that was played followed in broad outline the physical movements of the two pets, the bird and the puma, in the amusing performance we witnessed when we called upon Radiant Wing. The music rose and fell, as it were, in imitation, or emulation, of what was taking place between the two, together with the many sudden twists and turns, first this way, then that way. Beyond this, it is not feasible to go, in *words*, except that the piece was in every respect a *scherzo*, as might be rightly supposed from the nature of its 'programme'.

At the end of the playing Ruth expressed her delight, as did we all, especially Franz, who paid its composer the very sincere tribute of a brother artist.

'Now about the orchestral arrangement,' said Ruth; 'when shall we be able to hear that?'

'Very shortly, I hope,' Peter replied. 'It will be included in a programme of other works, of course. Shall I let you know?'

'Most certainly, please.' Roger had been standing with his back to the bookshelves while the music was being played; now he turned, and was to be observed reading the titles upon the volumes. Ruth and I joined him, feeling that at any moment he would make an interesting discovery.

The works were arranged in orderly manner according to their nature, with all the compositions written while Peter was on earth grouped together. He ran his forefinger along the titles, naming them over to himself. Suite in G, he read; Symphony No. 6, when Peter said: 'That work is always announced as "the last work the composer wrote". That is the line of demarcation, Roger, between what I wrote on earth and what I have done since.'

It was plain to see that the latter heavily outweighed the former by innumerable volumes.

'Yet this is nothing,' he continued; 'it is the same with all of us. Take Franz Joseph, there, he has written volumes and volumes of music. Opus numbers run into four figures here, Roger, and if we hadn't wonderful memories, we should be at a loss to know how much we had actually composed.'

'Is it easier to compose music here or on earth?' asked Roger.

'Oh, here, without a shadow of doubt. Consider how free we are from everything that might be—and so often was—a hindrance. Franz mentioned starvation, for instance. Call it plain hunger in this case, and all that it means. In other words, caring for the necessary bodily wants. We're entirely free of that. Public apathy—there's something else that's thankfully missing here. Difficulty of getting one's works heard or acknowledged. No trouble about that either—here. Somewhere pleasant to live: this little place is an example. Franz lives in a delightful house where he is as happy "as the day is long"—and it's a very long day here, Roger, as I expect you've noticed. Now what else is there?'

'No music critics,' said Franz with a chuckle, 'though fortunately for me I did not suffer much from those peculiar people. Not, I would have you understand, that my music was so perfect, but because I lived at a period when musical criticism was not the subject for every ignoramus who thinks he knows something about music, as I believe is the custom now on earth. Your native land was very kind to me, my friends, and still is,' he said, addressing the three of us by the bookshelves.

'And to me, too,' said Peter, 'though they *will* look on us as dead. Only think what a sensation we should cause, my dear Franz, if we could collect the rest, and go marching upon some concert platform on earth, one after the other, or arm-in-arm. There would be a riot. Think of the money we should make, or somebody would make out of us.'

'The second is more likely,' exclaimed Franz. 'Then the critics would begin operations. They would cut our symphonies and things into small pieces, and put them under the musical microscope; show us exactly where we went wrong, what we ought to have done, and what we were thinking about when we wrote them. And nobody would be able to understand a word any of them said, least of all themselves. But they would all be completely satisfied, and fancy themselves to be vastly superior people. No; I don't think it would be so amusing after all. It's safer here. We're among friends, we are free of all troubles and cares, especially that awful bugbear, the fear of writing ourselves out. We can always have a hearing whenever we wish, without going hat-in-hand to some objectionable fellow who wants to exploit us. And it's nice to be among ourselves as composers and musicians, and be pleasantly rude to each other with the greatest good will in the world, and knowing that no unpleasant intent is involved. It's a pity there are no composers to speak of, on earth, at present.'

'Are there any at all?' asked Franz.

'It seems a good many years since any came to join us here,' replied Peter; 'what do you say, Monsignor?'

'Well——' I began, but Ruth stepped in.

'You know, Peter,' she said, 'that given half a chance, Monsignor will let fly. Ever since he first became acquainted with all of you, and came under your combined tuition for practical purposes, some of the practical purposes have taken the form of outspoken words about the earth's present composers.'

'It's this way' I explained amid the laughter that Ruth caused, 'if I am to give a true picture of this world, I must speak the truth. Obvious and elementary, but so it is. The fact is that there are *no* master-composers at this moment on earth. I say that advisedly and without qualification. The composers at present there living are not worthy of the name. You truly observed, Peter, that it's a good many years since any real composers came to join us here. Composers have undoubtedly come here, but they were compelled to leave their musical monstrosities behind them. And there are others yet to come-and the same thing will happen to *them*.

'You know they say on earth that all spiritual revelation has ceased. The same folk would be speaking the truth if they said that the composing of pure music has ceased.' 'We have heard about it,' said Peter, 'but is it really as bad as all that? The music, I mean.'

'It is indeed. I've not exaggerated. Ruth will bear me out; she's heard some of it. And Roger has only recently left the earth. Did you ever listen to any of what the earth people call "modern" music, Roger?'

'I did—but not for long. It was more than I could stand.'

'We have heard about it from time to time,' Peter remarked, 'but never suspected that it was as terrible as you say. What do the beloved critics say about it?'

'Beautiful things: they hail it as the work of great geniuses, and bamboozle the public into thinking that the particular piece they're reviewing is full of lovely melodies, when it would take more than a searchlight—if you know what that is, my dear friend—and a microscope to find even the slightest trace of one. It's impossible to discover what isn't there. It is the same with art. You've no possible notion of the appalling daubs that are bought at the most fantastic prices for public exhibition. To say that they are nightmarish is to put it mildly.'

'But how do you account for their acceptance?'

'Perhaps upon two grounds: either a form of insanity, or a huge hoax. But the same acceptance is given for the revolting pictures as for the revolting music. That is the way of the earth at the moment—the cult of the hideous, the monstrous, the gigantically ugly. The poison has seeped its way into all the fine arts.'

'Dear me,' said Franz, 'I am glad we are out of it, and none too soon by what you say, Monsignor!'

We were amused by Franz's remarks, since he has been many years in the spirit world, long before the present decadence began to assail the arts. Peter Ilyitch has also been some considerable time here.

Peter came and stood beside Roger, who had resumed reading the titles of the music scores.

'May I take one down?'

'By all means, my dear fellow. Do what you like here,' Peter replied. 'No formalities, you know.' 'I know, sir; Monsignor and Ruth are always telling me, but I've not got altogether into the way of it yet.'

'It will come with practice, Roger,' smiled Peter. 'Begin now.'

'It is pretty marvelous. Everything, I mean. You know they have been showing me round, and everybody's so awfully decent. Kind, I mean. You get the feeling that you're the most important person when you're being shown anything. And Ruth and Monsignor seem to have wasted a terrible lot of time on me.'

'Not wasted, Roger; not wasted,' said Peter. 'Never that. Nobody ever wasted time here, because there's no time to waste! That sounds ambiguous doesn't it? Might mean anything '

'Here is something you must know, Roger,' I said, taking one of the scores from the shelf. 'Do you read music at all?'

'Not very well, I'm afraid.'

'Well, then, see if you recognize this tune.' I hummed an air known the world over, much to the amusement of Peter.

'Good gracious,' cried Roger, 'that's from——'

'From the book Monsignor is holding,' said Peter. I passed the volume to Roger, who looked from the music to Peter, then turned to the first page where he read the title and composer's name, and appeared rather breathless.

Franz, from his seat on the couch, watched what was going forward. 'So Roger,' said he, 'you have discovered his awful secret at last. Does he, do you think, come up to expectation? Or did you expect someone far handsomer— like myself, for instance?'

'The point is, can one be handsome and clever?' asked Peter.

'Oh, yes, there's no doubt of that,' returned Franz. 'I need not tell you where to look. Just use your own judgment. I shan't blush.'

'Well, Roger. We said you would have some surprises, and we've kept our word. Now, I think we must be off. Word has come that someone is on his way to see me. So we'll make for the house.'

We thanked Peter warmly for his 'hospitality', and Ruth reminded him of the new scherzo. He promised to let us know when it was to be performed orchestrally, and said that he would call for us, when we might all go together to hear and see the first public performance. As we walked through the woods, Roger expressed his delight and amazement that it should be so simple a matter to be able to talk and joke with a man whose name is a household word in the realm of music, in both worlds. 'Franz Joseph is equally well known, Roger,' said Ruth. 'He's an amazing man. He wrote more than a hundred symphonies when he was on earth.'

# Two Visitors

'I'VE noticed,' remarked Roger, 'that no one seems to use surnames here. I don't know even yours, or Ruth's.'

We had returned to our home directly following upon our visit to the house in the forest, and our conversations there with our two friends had evidently set up a train of thought in the mind of our protege.

'Why, no, Roger,' I replied, 'that is so; but then our surnames have no significance in this world. In fact, to the new arrival, there might almost appear to be some irregularity in the employment of names generally; no fixed custom or order about it. Here it is always a matter of personal identity, and not family identity.

'There is at least one fixed order of names here, and that is with the names that are of purely spirit world origin; names that are formed or built up in accordance with rules. Each one of them has a distinct meaning, and belongs to no earthly language. Names of that kind are given after they have been earned, and are only to be obtained through beings of the highest realms.

'As far as identity goes, you might take our Ruth as an example. Everyone hereabouts—and in many other quarters—knows her as Ruth, and it's a recognizable earthly name, as are many others.

'Mine is a designation, rather than a name, and on earth is an ecclesiastical title. You will recall that I mentioned that we have no titles here. This is no breaking of the rule, because the title, Monsignor, which I held on earth, is always used by *itself*, and never with my name conjoined to it. Our friends on earth started it, though they do sometimes use my Christian name. So the word Monsignor is impersonal as a title, but attached to me as a name for practical reasons.'

'I noticed neither of you bothered to know my surname,' said Roger.

'That is so. There's no need. You're already known as Roger, as you have seen for yourself.'

'The same thing applies to Franz Joseph and Peter Ilyitch, does it?'

'The same, exactly. We've simply lopped off their surnames, and they're not a scrap the worse off. What's most important is that no one complains about the custom, or rule, if you like to call it that. Everybody's happy.

'Do you remember, Roger, when we were chatting about age and identity, the difference that returning to the prime of life might make in one's personal appearance, so that a person might not be recognized for the individual he once was. Names will have something of the same effect, as you can see.

'When the higher personages go to the earth to speak to friends there, they are usually known by some name that has been specially chosen or invented for them. We have a very case in point. You heard me say to Peter and Franz that word .had reached me that someone wished to see me?'

'Yes; I thought perhaps you were making an excuse for coming away.'

'Roger,' protested Ruth; 'what *would* the earth folk say if they thought that telling fibs was the common practice in "heaven" for ending social calls?' 'As a matter of fact, old fellow, we don't need to tell them—which saves one an awful lot of worry and fuss.'

'Then what would you do if you wanted to get away from anywhere because you were a bit sick of it?'

'I can't say that situation has ever arisen that I know of. What do you say, Ruth? Can you recall any such?'

'No,' Ruth answered, 'I can't say I do. We never seem to have such awkward situations.'

'Because, my dear, they don't exist—and couldn't. No boredom, no question of outstaying one's welcome. All this, Roger, arises from your suspicion that we were telling whoppers so as to get away from Peter and Franz gracefully. The fact is that while we were there a message was "flashed" to me, that was all. It was not urgent, otherwise I shouldn't be gossiping here like this. The message came from someone who constantly visits the earth to speak to many friends there, and as we were upon pleasure rather than business I responded at once that we were available. Had the message come when Ruth' and I were upon "escort duty", the same kind as we performed for you, Roger, I should have sent back word of what we were doing, and in no circumstances would we have been expected to place ourselves at the disposal of anyone else, *however illustrious*. On the contrary, we should more likely get into trouble for leaving our work of the moment. Everything works upon lines of sound common sense and reason in these lands, Roger.'

'Pity it doesn't do the same on earth,' observed Roger, dryly.

'You may well say that. The visitor I'm telling you about is an eminent personage from the high realms, but his identity has been concealed under the simple yet effective name of Blue Star, and it's derived in a sensible, straightforward fashion from the fact that part of his personal insignia, if I may call it so, consists of a magnificent jewel, made in the form of a star of brilliant blue precious stones, more precious, my Roger, than anything that could be found or made upon earth. We'll ask him to show it to you when he comes .'

'He doesn't wear it always, then?'

'Not always in these realms, not visibly, that is.'

Being seated before one of the windows I was in a position to observe our visitor the moment he made his appearance in the garden. Roger guessed my reasons for so seating myself, for he asked, 'Is it customary for people on visits to come the long way round? I mean, to walk through the grounds rather than "think" themselves into the room?'

'Yes, Roger. That is the method we've employed all along in the few calls we've made round about. There's no law about it, you know; merely what good sense and good taste dictate. If the need for one's presence were vitally urgent, then we might use the thought method of getting us wherever we wanted to be, and so appear right in a person's presence without delay. But in all ordinary circumstances we behave like ordinary folk, and so present ourselves, walking upon our two legs, and, if necessary, we should knock on the front-door—though I don't ever remember doing that part of it.

'You'll find, Roger, as you go on, that you'll instinctively do the right thing. So don't let that detail trouble you. Calling upon our friends on earth is a different matter altogether. We went very quickly to your room to fetch you, and there were no formalities about knocking to be let in. If we had knocked, and by some chance your people had heard us, they would have been terrified, I expect.'

'I should think they would. Most likely thought I was making a dreadful end, and that someone worse than the old gentleman with the scythe had come to take me away.'

'Ah, here is our visitor, and he's not alone,' I said, as I perceived two people walking through the garden.

'Who can the other be?' Ruth remarked, as she came over to the window.

In a moment they drew sufficiently near to be recognized.

'Why, it's Phyllis,' Ruth cried, and hurried out into the garden.

'Ruth and Phyllis are old friends,' I explained to Roger, and then went to greet them.

'Well, my children,' said Blue Star; 'we were on our way to do a little work with our earth friends, and this young lady suggested that we make a detour, and pay a call. You were not at home when you received my message, I understand.'

'No, Blue Star. We had taken our friend to see Franz and Peter.'

'Ah, yes, that is good.'

'Could you spare a moment to see Roger? I've been telling him about you.'

'Not revealing all my dreadful secrets, I hope,' said Blue Star with a laugh.

'Come along in and meet Roger,' said Ruth to Phyllis; 'he's such a nice boy. He was our last "case", and now we're having a holiday together showing him the sights.'

There was a marked contrast between the two girls, for Phyllis has dark hair, while Ruth's is a bright golden. Roger rose as we entered the room, and I presented him to Blue Star and Phyllis.

'Well, my son,' said Blue Star, 'you look happy and well, and that is not surprising, is it?'

'No, sir,' the lad replied with a smile.

'Call me Blue Star. Everybody does; and why not? It's my name, after all—or one of them. Some of us have several names. On earth, I believe, if one has too many names one is apt to be regarded with suspicion, but here it is different. The name I had on earth has caused the most trouble, I fancy. But that is not *my* fault, but the fault of the people who have used it a shade too freely.'

Blue Star smiled. His voice had a soft timbre, and he spoke carefully, it seemed to me, and with deliberation. Young though he looked in years, yet his voice revealed a man whose advent into spirit lands had come centuries ago. It is a distinctive quality that makes itself apparent to the practised ear, where all outward signs of the ravages of earthly time have long since vanished. I learnt very early in my life here, that to try to assess people's ages is a dangerous task!

'I wonder, Blue Star, if I might ask a favour of you,' I said, 'for our young friend here?'

'Certainly, Monsignor. If it's possible for me to grant it, you have but to ask.'

'We have been telling Roger about names here, and I explained the origin of your own.'

'And now you wish a practical demonstration, and to see the origin—is that it ?'

Blue Star threw open one half of the rich cloak he was wearing, and displayed upon the inner garment the superb star that we had described to Roger.

'Come close, my son, and examine it properly. It is very beautiful, isn't it. I doubt if you have ever seen anything like this on earth, eh ?'

'Oh, *impossible*, Blue Star.'

'You see the wonderful characteristics of spirit world precious stones, my son. They need no reflected light; their lustre, their brilliance come from within themselves. If you could, by some means, take this star, or any other jewel, into the dark it would shine out like the sun in beautiful colour. Monsignor, I believe, has described it as "living light". That is absolutely so. The jewels on earth, lovely as they are, rely upon reflected light for their beauty and their effect. Take a priceless diamond, shall we say, into the dark on earth, and all its glory is gone. There are many, many other wonderful jewels in the spirit world besides this one, my son, and all of them made of this same "living light". As I expect you know by now, these cannot be bought in the spirit world.'

'No, Blue Star; I understand that. Monsignor and Ruth have told me a great deal already.'

'No buying and selling here; only earning. And isn't that true justice? It places us all upon an equal footing, and each of us has the same level chance to earn many wonderful things — like this blue star, for instance. Has Monsignor told you much about these jewels?'

'No, Blue Star, nothing,' I interposed. 'It wasn't until your message came that the subject cropped up.'

'The only reason I asked is because one doesn't want to tell you what you know already. Well, then, my son, I expect you wonder what they represent. In strict truth, they represent nothing but their own worth and beauty. They are what we would call adjuncts to our life, and are personal rewards for various services rendered.'

'Something like the orders they have on earth.'

'Something, my son, but not much! You see, these are not the insignia or jewels of exclusive orders, such as I understand exist on earth. Here they are open to all, without discrimination, who care to earn them, and they are not for certain privileged people as the custom is in some cases on earth. We carry no letters after our names because we are holders of such awards. That, I think, is a good idea, because some of our names would appear very odd decorated in that way; and then there is no call for us to proclaim that we are holders of such an award.

'You are fond of beautiful things, I can see, my son, since you find infinite delight even in this one example of spirit world beauty. You did not, by chance, see the jewels that Franz Joseph and Peter have? No, of course not. They would hardly show them to you unless you asked them. They and their brothers in art have many exquisite examples among them. All for services they have rendered to us here with their grand music. Why, now, I seem to be doing a great deal of talking. Is it a good habit, I wonder, or a bad one? What do you say, Monsignor?'

'Well, Blue Star, it can be a bad one; not here, I admit, but on earth, especially if one says the wrong things, as I did, from many a pulpit!'

Blue Star laughed. 'I can say I do a fair share of talking now, on earth,' he said. 'There is one thing people cannot accuse us of here: that we get too talkative in our old age. I expect, Roger, at first, you felt you could hardly speak at all as the wonders of these lands were unfolded to you by our friends.'

'That is so, Blue Star. I've mostly felt tongue-tied, or else kept my mouth closed, and eyes and ears open.'

'An admirable thing to do on occasion, my son. When we were on earth some of us spoke when it would have been better and wiser to have remained silent, and some of us remained silent when we should have spoken.'

'I am guilty under both counts, Blue Star !'

'Are you, indeed, Monsignor?' said Blue Star smiling. 'The person I was thinking of was not you, but myself! Now, Roger, you will never guess where Phyllis and I are going when we leave here, which must be in a moment or so, for time draws on. Ah, that surprises you, doesn't it? How can time draw on? Not here, but on earth, whither we are bound. Monsignor often comes with us, but not on this occasion. We are to journey to some friends on earth where Phyllis and I, and others, will exercise our awful propensity for talking, and try to cheer our earthly friends. Goodness knows, they need cheering—the whole earth needs it. And the people there could have it, if only they would all turn to us. It's a grey old place the earth, eh, Roger, after this brightness and colour?'

'One day,' said Phyllis, 'we'll take you to see our earth friends. Do you think you would like that, Roger?' Phyllis asked with a captivating smile.

'I'm afraid I don't know much about that sort of thing,' Roger replied with evident caution.

'No of course you don't. You can't expect to discover everything in five minutes, can you? You wouldn't have to go alone, you know. There's any number of us, and we usually go in a party.'

'I rather think that Phyllis has a particular partiality for parties,' said Blue Star with a laugh.

'Franz and Peter and others from the musical quarter often go with us. And Radiant Wing, too, and heaps more.'

'Not to mention old Blue Star, himself,' said our eminent visitor.

'Blue Star, don't say *old*,' said Phyllis indignantly.

'Thank you, my dear child, but my comparison with the rest of this present distinguished company, I am not exactly a youth.'

'I expect you feel like one,' said Roger.

'Ah, yes; that's another thing. Now, my child, we must really be off. It has been very pleasant to have this little idle chat with you all, though doubtless, according to earthly notions, we should have been discussing deep, deep questions that no one here wants to discuss at all, and trying to explain things that have no explanation. It would have been highly edifying, but extremely dull. I much prefer our own brand of small gossip. It's more entertaining, and I am sure it will do us much more good.'

And so with a wave of the hand our two visitors left us on their journey earthwards.

# The Ruler of the Realms

'WHAT is so astonishing,' observed Roger, 'is that there don't seem to be any signs of government anywhere.'

'Would that be a complaint, Roger, or a compliment?'

'Certainly not a complaint.'

'Then we'll take it as a compliment. No, however hard you look, you'll see no signs whatever of any form of government. It is there, none the less. I dare say you were thinking in terms of legislatures, acts of parliament, by-laws, orders-in-council, decrees, and many more horrors of ordered life on earth.

'Now I'll ask you a question, Roger. Have you seen anywhere notice-boards or notices telling you you must not do this or that, or informing you what the office hours are, or warning you with the old, familiar "trespassers will be prosecuted", or even "keep off the grass"?'

'No, not one—anywhere.'

'And you never will, for they don't exist here. Unique, don't you think ?'

'Very much so.'

'From which you will gather,' said Ruth, 'that we are all beautifully behaved.'

'The truth is, my boy, that our "government" is by natural laws, and therefore the best in the whole universe. Better, a million times, than anything that could ever be devised from man's ingenuity. Natural laws need no enforcing; they enforce themselves.

'The natural laws on earth are not so easily perceived. Few, for instance, can see the natural law at work when thoughts are emitted. We can here, and their effect. Obviously, some of those laws have no effect whatever on earth. If you had tried to shift your physical body by the power of thought, as you are able to do now, Roger, you would have remained where you were. Still, the natural laws are not the only means of what might be called government here. We have rulers.'

'That's more what I was thinking when I asked you about governments.'

'Each realm has its ruler. That's not a strictly accurate term, though we do use it.'

'Doesn't he rule then?'

'No that's just it. He doesn't. He presides, and that is very different. I'm talking about the realms of light now. You can see for yourself how much pleasanter and easier it makes life. No failing of one government merely to make way for another equally bad or stupid or ineffective. No political fanatics with insane and inane ideas, and, what is most important, no individuals holding office who are totally unfitted for it. If the people of earth would like to settle some of their worst problems, the spirit world could give them a hint or two on how to do it.'

'Monsignor is now getting on to a subject where he would like to have one of his pulpits back,' said Ruth.

'I would, indeed, my dear; but suppose it were possible, suppose for one moment it could be done, how many would heed a word I could say? Why they would not take a scrap of notice of the wisest heads in the whole spirit world. Small use for me, then.

'Some of us, as you know, are in pretty close touch with events and affairs on the old earth, Roger, and some of us can see which way they are drifting. Can you not imagine, then, how the great beings in the highest realms must regard the situation, when supreme wisdom is to be had for the asking, if only incarnate man were not so blind?

'Look how the Churches are wasting their time and energies upon the sheerest trivialities. It is all so pitiable and dreadful. You've seen a little of this world, Roger, and one or two people in it. You're young, and fresh from the earth. You can surely see that the spirit world is right, and the earth world is wrong in so many things. Isn't the course a simple one as it presents itself to your mind?'

'You're perfectly right, Monsignor. It does look simple— *from this side of life.*'

'Have things changed so much, then, since I was on earth, would you say?'

'I can't say from my own experience, you know, Monsignor,' Roger said with a smile, 'because you were there before my time. But from what I've heard people say, there's been a lowering of standards in many ways on earth.'

'They cannot have gone up very high if the best that can be done is to produce two world wars, and then talk about a third. And what about the Churches?'

'Oh, they still disagree among themselves.'

'Precisely. All this springs from your mention of government over here. I was telling you about the rulers who preside over the realms. Many of them have been living here thousands of years. It requires the highest attributes to become one: for example, knowledge of humanity and sympathy, understanding, and discretion; patience, kindness, and spirituality. Those are a few that are demanded. A ruler's knowledge is prodigious. At least that is how it would appear to earthly eyes, but you know now, Roger, how memories work here. It's safe to say that the ruler of a realm has a vast knowledge of the people under his care, and that is what makes him so very different from other folk. For one thing, the rulers belong to realms higher than those over which they preside.

'But over, and above, the rulers is one who is the greatest of them all, and he is the ruler of all the realms of the spirit world.'

We were sitting in a 'back' room during this conversation, when we heard a familiar voice calling: 'May we come in?'

'That's Omar's voice,' Ruth cried, and we jumped up and ran to the door. Omar it was, and with him his constant companion, the Egyptian.

'This is a surprise, Omar! Have you come on business or pleasure, or both?' 'Oh, pleasure,' replied Omar; 'business only ages one, so I avoid it as much as possible. That is what keeps me young. How is Roger?'

Roger being very able to answer for himself, did so: 'Wonderful,' said he.

'And you look it, my son. That is capital. The medicine has done you good, and the patient is now fully restored. Well, now to the real purpose of my call. I have a message for you to say that as my "master" is coming to this realm shortly, he would be pleased if he might visit you for a moment. There, that is my commission; simple and brief. I think I can guess your answer.'

'It needs no guessing, Omar. This is a private visit, I take it—to the realm, I mean?'

'Oh, yes; at least, as private as one can make it, and that's not easy, as you know.'

'This is splendid news, Omar. I need not say how grateful we are, and especially am I happy on account of our youngster, here.'

We exchanged a few more pleasantries, and Omar and his companion took their departure.

'Roger,' I said, 'this is something I never expected would happen so soon, though, in truth, one never knows.'

'Who is this personage that's coming? he inquired.

'Do you remember you once asked us if we knew how old the spirit world is, and that we told you about one being, at least, who was in existence himself before the earth was? You remember, of course. Well, it is he who is coming, and incidentally, it is he who is the ruler of all the realms of the spirit world, that I spoke about only a moment ago.

'You know, Roger, there are folk on earth who believe that the beings of the highest realms never by any chance leave those realms, because it would be too appallingly distasteful for them to leave the rarefied state in which they live. That is absolutely wrong. Those marvellous beings can, and do, journey into the different realms. It sometimes transpires that an individual may be speaking to one such personage and be totally unaware of it.'

'Who is this being,' Roger asked again; 'surely not——?'

'I know what you were going to say, my boy. No, he is not the Father of the universe, though one can understand the inference you might be tempted to draw even from the little we've told you.

'He is known by sight, Roger, to every single soul living in the realms of light. How many thousands there are who name him as their "beloved master"—and that includes Omar him-self—it is impossible to say.

'He exercises over all the realms the function that the individual ruler exercises over the realm to which he is ap-pointed. He unifies the whole of the realms of the spirit world into one gigantic universe, over which reigns the Father us all. You cannot have the remotest conception, my Roger, of the magnitude, the immensity of the powers possessed by him, and yet, with it all he is the most gracious being it is possible to contemplate. His position is one of absolute regality, if one can so term it, while he himself is indescribable.

'You will be able to judge for yourself, very soon, the enormous degree of knowledge, spirituality and wisdom he possesses. The colours denoting these three attributes are blue, white, and gold, and he has them upon his robe in enormous proportions. You saw for yourself how Omar has these three colours in no inconsiderable degree himself. Even so, there is this still greater.'

'This is a little frightening, Monsignor, to put it mildly. I was rather used to taking a back seat when I was on earth, and this looks like another occasion when it might be advisable to do it again. In other words, bolt before your visitor arrives.'

'No, no, no, Roger. Stay, stay, you must.'

'At any rate, I might be in the way.'

'Oh, come, Roger, my dear,' interposed Ruth, 'you've stayed with us so far, and our advice has been good, though I do say so.'

We had got thus far in our deliberations when we per-ceived two old friends walking across the grass, for we had remained out of doors after the departure of Omar and the Egyptian. The present callers were none other than Franz Joseph and Peter Ilyitch. Cordial greetings were exchanged, and we hastened to tell them of Omar's visit and its purpose.

'Of course, you will both remain?' I concluded.

'My dear friend,' said Franz, 'you would have some difficulty in trying to dislodge either of us.'

'Roger feels a little nervous,' I told them.

'Dear me,' said Peter; 'that won't do. Still, I can understand. Now I'll tell you what to do, Roger. Wait until he comes, and then if you feel "stage-fright" coming over you, well, you know the method of quickly removing yourself. But you won't. The minute you see this visitor, you will *want* to stay. That's how Franz and I felt on our first occasion of seeing him. We have seen him many times since, and spoken with him. We have so much to be thankful for, as it is from his high realm that the arts derive their inspiration, even to reaching as far as the earth. Many of us, since we came here, have had the opportunity to acknowledge and be grateful for what was given to us in those days on earth. Isn't that so, Franz, old friend?'

'Indeed, it is. We little knew on earth whence our ideas were coming.' Ruth, meanwhile, had placed a rather handsome armchair in the main room, a task that she always insisted upon assuming to herself upon all such occasions. As we assembled before the house, we could perceive a distinct brightening of the light upon the outskirts of our small 'estate', and we knew this for an unmistakable sign that our visitors were near. We therefore walked down the wide path that is flanked by broad beds crammed with flowers of many colours, and which led directly from the house towards where we should meet our visitors. Another moment, and we saw them approaching. Our guest was walking with Omar and the

Egyptian upon either side of him, the latter carrying a large bouquet of superb white roses. This, as we discovered later, was composed of a number of small bouquets. Omar was the first to speak.

'Well, my dear friends,' said he, 'we meet again, and Franz is here, and Peter. That is well.'

Our visitor took the hands of each of us, and spoke a word of kindly greeting. Franz and Peter had each taken an arm of Roger to give him assurance, and the picture presented by this action at once amused our visitor, for it chanced that our two friends had taken a somewhat firm hold upon Roger's arms.

'What is this, my children?' he laughed. 'You look to be holding the boy to prevent his escape from us.'

Ruth explained that Roger was a little nervous, since his experience was so far rather limited.

'Come, now, Roger, my child,' he said, 'what is there to fear? Would you be fearful of me? Give me your hand—so. Now banish hence all fears, never to return. It sounds like an incantation, doesn't it?'

Roger's confidence was restored immediately, and he was himself once more. 'I think it will be safe now to release your prisoner, Peter and Franz.'

The two appeared somewhat confused because neither of them had realized, nor had Roger, that they were still linked in arms. The rest of us enjoyed this little episode, trifling enough in itself, but filled with kindness and humanity, and revealing, as clearly as the noonday sun, that even the highest personages from the highest realms of the spirit world are not impossible beings, grim and forbidding, humourless and unsmiling, but that they breathe forth the very essence of all that is warmhearted and human.

Roger never for an instant took his eyes from our illustrious guest, who was habited as he usually is upon such visits:

that is to say, in a gossamer-like white robe, bordered with a deep band of gold, over which he wore a rich cloak or mantle of brilliant blue, fastened by a great pink pearl. His hair was golden, though when this is seen in the high realm where he lives, the golden hue becomes golden light.

What seemed to attract Roger most of all was the countenance of our visitor, for following upon what we had told him of his immense *age*, as measured in earthly time, and running into millions of years, yet could Roger perceive no signs of the passage of time. Yet most assuredly when he spoke to Roger, the latter knew that there stretched behind him æons of time, while he presented the outward appearance of eternal youthfulness.

At length we repaired indoors; our guest seated himself in the special armchair, while we occupied a half-circle round him—seated also, I need hardly add, for upon all occasions we behave like rational human beings!

Our guest spoke to each of us in turn, and here again, lest I should be misunderstood, let me hasten to affirm that our conversation was also upon rational lines. We were most certainly not like a group of school-children being submitted to an awful inquisition by some bloodless inspector! We were free to speak when we wished, subject to the demands of ordinary good manners. And what is most important, we had many an occasion for laughter—and we laughed. No conversation could possibly be without humour where Omar is present, and he was capably aided and abetted both by Franz and Peter. Roger marvelled greatly at their apparent boldness, but he soon learned that did he wish to express his own thoughts upon any subject, he was expected to do so.

Our guest thanked the two composers for all their work, as well as that of their colleagues, and assured them of his ever continued help and inspiration. It was interesting—and to

Roger a revelation; another among so many—to hear the three discussing a number of musical technicalities with lively vigour. At last he spoke directly to Roger about his future, and astonished the boy by displaying much interest in, and especially knowledge of, his affairs. 'Information reaches me from many quarters,' he said; 'it was Omar who told me, and Monsignor who told Omar, that you have shown a keen interest in the creation of flowers.' Roger explained how we had visited the nursery-gardener, who had cordially invited him to join his pupils whenever he wished.

'That is good, my son. As you have seen for yourself, there is an abundance of useful things for you to do, the doing of which will bring great happiness to yourself, and provide for your progress and advancement through the realms of this world. You will have seen, too, my son, how we all perform our different tasks for the general welfare without thought of personal reward. Yet the rewards come none the less, lavish rewards—and so you will discover for yourself.

'Whenever you feel so disposed the work awaits you, but that is not to say you must curtail your present explorations. No one in these or other realms would wish—nor, indeed, would they have the right—to put a definite term upon your desires for knowledge gained at first hand in this way. But there does came a time when the activity of the mind is such that there is a compelling wish to be doing something actively rather than to be a mere witness passively, as it were, to what is going on around you.

'You will never want for wise and willing friends to help you in whatever way you need. You have already in this brief period, gathered friends about you, from whom nothing can separate you, for you now live in a world where no such separation can take place. We are always here, even as you are.

'If you wish to study music, or follow any of the other arts, we can promise you such teachers as the earth cannot provide, for here we have the masters, the real masters, two of whom, I am happy to see, are with us here.

'Then, Roger, my son, take up your new work whenever the inclination comes upon you, with the full knowledge that: the work performed in this world is never wasted effort.

'Now, my friends, the time has come for us to leave. Before doing so, I would like to leave a little memento of our visit.' Here the Egyptian passed into his hands the bouquet of roses.

'Accept these, my friends, with my love and blessings. Perhaps, Roger, you will help to create some roses as lovely as these. Remember me when you do so, and you shall have my thoughts, for the white rose is my favourite flower. Our friends here have seen them flourishing in my own gardens. I think, Omar,' he concluded, 'we will return at once. And so, my dear children, the blessings of the Father upon you, and my love remain with you.'

So saying, our guests took their departure.

'Well, Roger, my dear fellow,' I said, after a moment had elapsed, 'aren't you glad you stayed?

'Aren't you glad we didn't let you get away?' said Peter and Franz together.

But Roger was unable to 'come to earth' for a while. When he did, he was sufficiently wild with excitement to take us each in turn and 'waltz' us round the room. Both Franz and Peter being equally elated, seated themselves at the piano, where they instantly played a duet with great zest, while Ruth and Roger continued to dance throughout the apartment.

At length, we became a little less boisterous, though the feeling of elation is such on these occasions that some form of outlet becomes a positive necessity.

What we had enjoyed was no 'spiritual experience', such as the religiously-minded on earth might consider it to be. An overwhelming experience, it would be foolish to deny, and its spiritual value it would be equally foolish to ignore, but the emotions we felt were deliriously bright, cheerful, happy, exhilarating emotions; never pious or sanctimonious, nor so awe-inspiring as to leave us bereft of all sense of complete enjoyment-for the latter is what was intended by the visit, and not something done solely for the 'good of our immoral souls'. Those same immortal souls would derive superabundant benefit in a natural way, without overlaying it with unnatural, impossible religiosity.

Hence, then, our 'exuberance of spirits'—in more senses than one—and hence, also, the way in which we demonstrated it, and were completely unashamed in the doing thereof.

We continued to talk for some long while after our three visitors had left, and we discussed with Roger his now expressed wish to begin work with the gardener, while between times he could pursue his explorations on all such occasions as he felt inclined. We assured him that were either Ruth or I engaged upon our own work at such periods, he would not lack ciceroni to take our places. Indeed, both Franz and Peter offered to deputize for us whenever required. .

Nothing therefore remained to be done but to apprise our gardener friend of the advent of a new pupil.. This was at once put in hand put in a simple fashion by our setting out in a body for the nursery, where a great welcome was accorded Roger, together with many assurances that in a brief space he would soon learn to create many beautiful flowers in general, and white roses in particular, which was now his one, over-powering desire.

# Epilogue

OUR rambles and visits were temporarily halted when Roger became a student at the nursery-garden, and at first we saw little of him. He quickly gained proficiency, as two fine white rose-trees, standing one on each side of the wide path before our house, give eloquent testimony. Thereafter he relaxed his studies somewhat, and we were able to forgather more often, subject to the exigencies of our own work. He has established a study for himself upon the upper floor of our home, replete with technical volumes, where, at the present moment, he is engaged upon a close study of a particularly intricate floral formation.

He is also occupied upon some horticultural plans based upon careful measurements which he took of our own small domain, from which Ruth and I deduce that the gardens round about our home will in due season undergo considerable alteration and rearrangement, an achievement to which we look forward with pleasurable anticipation.

The friends he has made have derived benefit in numerous ways from Roger's newly acquired skill. Radiant Wing reports that a quantity of the most colourful and perfectly formed flowers are now enhancing his own gardens, and several suggestions made by Roger have been carried out with eminent success, within the gardens themselves, to the great satisfaction of their owner.

Both Franz Joseph and Peter Ilyitch are in constant receipt of exquisite posies and bouquets of flowers for the further adornment of their respective homes, while Peter avers that the grounds around his house in the forest have lately come beneath Roger's speculative eye, and to his manifest delight, Peter has invited him to accept carte-blanche in carrying out whatever 'improvements' he wishes to make.

Our friend who lives in the cottage has not been neglected, and Roger is a frequent visitor there, the two having become fast friends. I would like to make it perfectly clear, lest misunderstanding should arise, that our young friend Roger, the brief chronicle of whose life so far in these lands of the spirit world, is the subject of these writings, is no imaginary person, created merely as a character upon whom to hang certain spiritual facts. He is a real person whose passing and immediately subsequent story are precisely as here recounted. That story is an excessively simple one, such as could be narrated of countless thousands of other young folk, of either sex, as well as of older people. It is in no way exceptional or unusual, and although Roger could be said to typify numberless others, none the less he is Roger, a young man of great charm, and of whom we all grow increasingly fond. His merry pranks and lightness of heart are our constant joy, while behind his gaiety are great kindliness, a firm determination, and a mind capable of deep thought. He is equally at home with those who can count many 'years' to their age as he is with the very young; for on numerous occasions he has accompanied Ruth and myself to the children's realm, where Ruth is always looked for eagerly both for herself and her musical accomplishments, and where I have gained some small reputation as a story-teller. Here, in this enchanting region, Roger is in his element among the little ones.

Such is the lad's enthusiasm for his work that he deems it his duty to entice Ruth and me into taking up the study of floriculture, in addition to our other occupations. Should he succeed in his efforts, we shall insist that Roger himself takes us as his pupils and teaches us the art of which he is now such a capable exponent. One last word remains: it is almost inevitable that the charge will be made that the modest experiences and the mild conversation that have been here recorded are so inconsiderable as to be of little moment in the great spiritual scheme of life 'hereafter', and that upon all occasions only matters of the highest importance and greatest application would ever be considered by 'discarnate beings'.

The spirit world is at all times a place where human beings can live in such comfort and happiness as they were meant to do *from the beginning*. We do not therefore spend our eternity in constant 'prayer and praise' because that as a mode of life would be no life at all, not even mere existence. We do not occupy our time—or waste it—in profound theological discussions upon obscure theories nor upon the more commonplace ones for the simple reason that we have something much better to do, in every way more profitable, and infinitely more entertaining and enjoyable. Our conversation is at all times rational, natural and normal. We do not speak to one another in terms of religious texts and scriptural quotations, nor are we endowed with wide knowledge and keen intellectual perception the instant we set foot in the spirit world at our dissolution. We are deeply thankful that we are ourselves and not as others would have us to be. And so to conclude: the friends who have passed before you in these pages have begged to conjoin themselves with me as I say to you:

Benedicat te oranipotens Deus.